friend
me

friend me

Donna Carter

WHITAKER
HOUSE

Dictionary definitions are taken from *Collins English Dictionary* online, 2012.

Some names and details have been altered slightly for purposes of privacy.

FRIEND ME:
Turning Faces into Lasting Friendships

Straight Talk Ministries
donnacarter.org
1.866.835.5827

The author is represented by
MacGregor Literary, Inc., of Hillsboro, Oregon.

ISBN: 978-1-60374-690-8
eBook ISBN: 978-1-60374-688-5
Printed in the United States of America
© 2013 by Donna Carter

Whitaker House
1030 Hunt Valley Circle
New Kensington, PA 15068
www.whitakerhouse.com

Library of Congress Cataloging-in-Publication Data (Pending)

1 2 3 4 5 6 7 8 9 10   19 18 17 16 15 14 13

DEDICATION

It seems appropriate to me to dedicate this book on friendship to the very first people with whom I found a profound sense of belonging: my family of origin. The nest in my family tree was safe, both physically and emotionally. It was full of nurture, truth, and fun. And when it was time to fly away, I could do so with confidence and competence because of the love and affirmation I had received there. The warm relationships associated with the nest keep drawing me back to stay engaged with the wonderful people God chose to be my family.

Mom and Dad, your example is undiluted by any falseness. I have never once doubted the authenticity of your love for God, for each other, or for your three daughters. Seeing Mom's faith expressed over a lifetime of service made serving God and people seem like the natural thing to do. Mom, if King Lemuel's mother had met you, she wouldn't have had to fabricate the virtuous woman described in Proverbs 31. You are my hero.

I have two sisters: Debbie, the "nice sister," so accepting and kind, is older; Jocelyn, the "fun sister" with the sparkling personality and big heart, is younger. I'm the middle sister with the identity crisis who thinks too much. Despite the usual childhood arguing and sibling rivalry that occurs in most families, I have long known that my sisters are beautiful women, and I love them dearly. I didn't know how fiercely they loved me until I arrived home safely after being evacuated by the Canadian Armed Forces from the rubble of Port-au-Prince, Haiti, after the 2010 earthquake there. I came through the sliding doors of the secure area of the airport, only to be nearly knocked down by the intensity of my precious sisters' hugs and sobs. I belong.

Now it seems Debbie has to leave us. Unless God performs a miracle, it will be soon. Often I find myself asking aloud, "How will we live without her?" And then I answer myself with the truth whispered deep into my heart: "With God's grace."

Debbie, all through your illness, you have denied my attempts to tell you how irreplaceable you are to me. But this is *my* book, darn it!—I can say whatever I want—so I am going to say it now.

Since I was a tiny girl, you were my safe place. I would have followed you anywhere. And I did. Into haunted houses and wild rides at the Calgary Stampede. On horseback and water skis. Doing things I never would have done, had I not adored you as I did. I followed you into a relationship with Jesus. You couldn't have been more than eight years old when you led me in a prayer to invite Jesus into my life. Later I followed you into ministry, and we enjoyed a wonderful synergy, blending your behind-the-scenes leadership gifts with my behind-the-microphone ones—kind of like Moses and Aaron. Then, an agonizing ministry experience drove us even closer together in spirit, though it drove us apart geographically. The parting was so difficult that we couldn't say good-bye without setting a date for the next time we would be together.

This time, that is impossible. I can't follow where you are going now, and I don't know when I will. This parting is so painful, I feel as though my arm is being severed from me, one inch at a time. This whole family has your cancer, and we weep while the tearing continues. And in your wise and gentle way, you grieve—not for yourself, because you know your glorious destination—but because your imminent departure causes us such pain. How you will be more beautiful in heaven is hard to imagine. One day, I won't have to imagine it. I will follow you. Until then, God's grace will be enough if we walk with Him moment by moment, day by day, in tear-stained joy. His grace is enough.

Though it appears I won't follow Debbie anytime soon, unless God heals you, Dad, you will. How can I express what your steadfast presence has meant in my life? You affirmed my femininity while instilling in me the firm belief that I could do anything I chose to do. Your tender strength prepared me to engage in healthy, hope-filled relationships with men and women alike. That bedrock of trust provided the foundation for the nurturing marriage Randy and I have enjoyed for more than thirty years.

Every day, you told your daughters that you loved us. Having a dad who was affectionate, protective, and involved made trusting God with my life an easy leap. Although our remaining time together on this earth is short, I will never outlive your imprint on my life. You leave a legacy of serving God with your time, gifts, and resources. And of loving your family so well.

I am keenly aware that I have a lot to lose only because I had so much to begin with. Though I grieve in this season of profound loss, I am so blessed. Mom, Dad, Debbie, and Jocelyn...I love you with my whole heart.

ACKNOWLEDGMENTS

Many people have invested in this book, and many more have invested in my life. My family and my dear friends Helene, Audrey, and Becky have been such a source of strength and encouragement to me through this process of writing and publishing. Your words, prayers, and hugs have meant the world. Thanks for taking a break from your own busy lives to check in on mine.

Don Bastian was the first publishing professional to take an interest in me. Thanks so much, Don, for the information, the affirmation, and the editing.

Thanks to my new friends at Whitaker House: Cathy, Christine, and Courtney. (Does your name have to begin with "C" to work there?) Your enthusiasm for this project put wind in my sails and a smile on my face. Thank you for your excellent work in marketing, coordinating, and editing, respectively.

Michelle, Karen, Heather, Patty and Marshall, Dave, John, Randy, Carla, Dale, Marilyn, Allan, Laura, Paula, Brenda, Kevann, Les, "The Chicks," Wendy, Shirley, Melanie, Theresa, Sandie, and Catherine—thank you for letting me tell your stories. Others will be richer for learning from them.

Finally, and especially, to the Delamont family: Brian, Darlene, Caleb, Daniel, and Michael (and now, Kendall Delamont). The way God has woven our lives and families together is an expression of His grace. Thanks for allowing me to tell this beautiful and intimate story for the benefit of others and the honor of God.

CONTENTS

PREFACE

Many people have relationships a mile wide and an inch deep. Social networking sites, such as Facebook, Twitter, and MySpace, enable us to keep in touch with hundreds of people. But do we really *know* those people? We read headline-style updates about their lives and witness their big moments in photo slideshows, but rarely do we see their hurts, know their dreams, or understand their needs. Many of us approach the latest technology in smartphones and iPads as time-efficient devices to help us manage our relationships while expending the smallest amount of energy.

There is no denying the convenience of social networking sites, and there's nothing wrong with using them to keep in touch with a broad range of people—family members, friends, co-workers, and so on. My husband has over a thousand "friends" on Facebook. However, he also has face-to-face friends with whom he shares the ups and downs of his life. We all need those people in our lives—friends who know our struggles and insecurities, who are familiar with our pains and our pasts—people who have probed the depths of our character over the long haul, who know it all and love us, anyway. We need friends who value us in our unmasked state and accept us as we are, yet also nurture us in our weakness and challenge us in our shortcomings. While it's true that our relationships are often the source of our deepest wounds, the fact remains that we were made for relationship— we need it to survive. The key is to establish "safe" friendships— places where we can be ourselves without fear of judgment or condemnation.

Friend Me is a tool to do just that. This book explores the barriers to "safe" friendship—for example, the fear of being known, the fear of rejection, feelings of jealousy or inferiority, and plain old busyness. We will discuss the characteristics of true friendship, as well as the indicators of toxic relationships, and explore how to safely navigate a relationship through calm and turbulent waters alike. We will also answer the question "How can I find a friend?" even as we acknowledge that there are times when God sees fit to let us experience periods of solitude or even isolation, for the purpose of drawing our attention to something inside of us or to another relationship, whether it's with another person or with our heavenly Father Himself. After all, He is the best Friend we can ever hope to have!

If you long for true friendship with more than face value, read on, and don't give up. The road may be hard, at times, but it's a journey well worth taking.

Some people come into our lives and quickly go.
Some stay for a while and leave footprints on our hearts.
And we are never, ever the same.
—Flavia Weedn

Part I

THE POWER OF FRIENDSHIP

1

JUST ONE FRIEND

My friends all thought they were there to help me celebrate my fortieth birthday—to have lunch, sing, eat cake, and laugh. But that wasn't why I had invited them to the restaurant. I had something quite different in mind. The poor waiter must have been confused by the whole event. One minute, he walked into the private dining room we occupied and found us laughing uncontrollably; when he came back, moments later, he found us all in tears.

Why had I arranged a gathering of my friends at the restaurant that day? Because I was determined not to repeat a mistake for which I was still struggling to forgive myself. On that day, I told my friends—all of the dear women who mean so much to me—how much I appreciated them, the specific ways in which each of them enriched my life, and how thankful I was that God had brought them into my life. I knew I might not have another chance....

⌒

I could hardly believe it. After twenty years of living at least half a continent away from each other, my dearest childhood friend, Sonja, and I would finally be living in the same neighborhood again. After years of missionary work in Europe and ministry elsewhere in Canada, Sonja, her husband, Brian, and their children were moving back to Calgary.

I first met Sonja when I was ten, and we were inseparable from that point forward. When we grew up and got married, she was my maid of honor, and I was hers. At my wedding reception, I introduced her with several lines from "Seasons in the Sun," a song by Terry Jacks that was popular then— specifically, the verse that reminisces about the joys of childhood friendships and the shared lessons of life and love learned in that season.

Shortly after our marriages, our paths diverged. And it wasn't until August 2000 that we were together again.

But there was a problem.

During Sonja's second pregnancy, thirteen years prior to our reunion, she had developed a pesky cough that wouldn't go away. The doctors suspected pneumonia. After performing some tests, they delivered some good news: Sonja was carrying twins. They also delivered some bad news: Sonja had cancer— specifically, a very aggressive cancer called non-Hodgkin's lymphoma.

She and Brian were stationed in Germany at the time, and because the doctors couldn't guarantee the effectiveness of the treatment protocol on a pregnant woman, they scheduled her for an abortion. Sonja and Brian both refused, and they brought their family back to Calgary, where she underwent aggressive chemotherapy, even though the doctors weren't sure how it would affect her unborn babies. Their speculation about deformities and other severe birth defects challenged Brian and Sonja's faith daily as Sonja endured the treatment and its side effects.

But the treatment seemed to be working. The twins were born three months premature, and, while they faced profound breathing problems and other issues common among preemies, they were otherwise healthy and whole. Immediately after the twins' cesarean birth, Sonja's radiation treatment began.

Only months after Sonja and her family returned to Germany, the cancer came back. So, it was to Canada again for further chemo, followed by a bone marrow transplant. The treatment was successful, in that Sonja was cured of cancer—yet the treatment also resulted in complications that now posed a new risk to her cancer-free body.

⌒

I met Sonja halfway through the school year in fifth grade at Mapleridge Elementary School, when she moved to the area with her family. I remember thinking that my new classmate looked very grown-up and very, very, groovy. Her hair was long, styled in a wavy shag, and her blue eyes peered somewhat shyly through her oval wire-rimmed glasses. She wore denim hip-huggers and a macramé belt. She was tall and curvy; I was skinny and, well, skinny. I was very impressed by this cool new girl, and I wanted to be her friend. So, I introduced myself. And our lives were forever changed.

A few weeks later, we were standing outside the school, talking, as usual, until we had to part ways. We couldn't walk home together because Sonja lived to the west of the school, while I lived to the east. That day, Sonja told me that her parents were getting a divorce. I felt sad for my friend. I couldn't imagine how I'd feel if my parents decided to separate.

I started inviting my new friend to attend various church activities with me, including girls' club, camp, and Sunday school. Sonja seemed happy to oblige, and it wasn't long before she made the decision to become a follower of Jesus. Faith in God was just one more thing we had in common. Beyond our shared interest in boys and books and clothes and music—and our mutual, alarming lack of athletic prowess—we now shared the unique bond of those who have given their lives to Jesus. What had been a close friendship became much more. We were, in the words of L. M. Montgomery's character Anne of Green Gables, "kindred spirits."

As Sonja's parents' divorce was finalized, Sonja's mom, Bonnie, decided that she wanted to get away from Calgary—away from her ex-husband, away from the memories, just away. She decided to move with her three girls to Lethbridge, a city about two hours south. Sonja and I were devastated. We couldn't bear the thought of not seeing each other every day. We moped and we mourned.

And then, the house across the street from mine went up for sale.

My bedroom window overlooked that brown bungalow, and I'll never forget the day Sonja and I knelt together at that window and prayed to God that Sonja would live in that house instead of moving to Lethbridge.

The next phase of our plan was to march up to the door of the house, knock, and request entrance, to find out whether it would be a suitable home. (We needed to gather some ammunition for our argument to Sonja's mom if we hoped to convince her that she should move six blocks away rather than leave the city altogether.) I can only imagine what the homeowner across the street thought when two twelve-year-old girls showed up to talk real estate.

The house was all wrong for Bonnie and her three girls. It had only three bedrooms, the basement had not been finished, and, most significant, it wasn't located in Lethbridge. Still, I knew it was meant for Sonja and her family.

> I can think of no greater gift in those early years of adolescence than having my best friend close by.

Bonnie bought the house. To this day, I don't know what made her change her mind and make such a radical change of plans. It must have had something to do with our childlike faith in a great God who loves to give good gifts to His children. For I can think of no greater gift in those early years of adolescence than having my best friend close by. Besides my family, Sonja was my whole world. To this day, I can't imagine what my teenage years might have been like without her.

Living across the street from each other enabled us to spend even more of our time together. Sonja became part of our family, and I part of hers. If she wasn't at my house, I was probably at hers. My other friends would actually phone Sonja's house and ask for me. More than once, I went along on a family vacation with Sonja, her sisters, and her mother. Maybe Bonnie wanted to avoid all of the hugs and tears that went on whenever we had to spend a week or two apart.

Living so close also meant that when I went to church, Sonja came, too. When my parents dragged me to girls' club, I dragged Sonja to girls' club; if I went to Bible camp, so did she. It was through these contacts that she learned to love God with her whole heart, grew a strong faith, and met a young man named Brian—with whom she eventually fell head-over-heels in love.

> I knew Sonja loved me for who I was, and I returned her unconditional love.

It was okay that I wasn't popular at school. It was okay if I was mocked for taking a stand when my faith demanded it. It was okay to say no to peer pressure. Because, at the end of the day, Sonja was still my friend; I always had someone to walk home with. Cool or uncool, cheerful or ill-tempered, succeeding with flying colors or failing miserably, I knew Sonja loved me for who I was, and I returned her unconditional love.

Our loyalty faced occasional challenges. When we were approaching our graduation from ninth grade (long before Sonja met Brian), Sonja secured a date to the festivities—a boy she'd met in band. I had no such prospects. Unwilling to leave such an important match up to chance, I mustered my courage and invited a high-school boy named John, whom I knew only slightly from church but had admired from afar.

He must have been flattered, because he agreed to go. Soon after, we started dating. Of course, everywhere I went with John, Sonja came along, because wherever there was a Donna, there was a Sonja, too.

Somewhere along the line, however, John's affections shifted. It turns out that I was the third wheel, not Sonja, and I didn't even know it. When I was on vacation, John made his interests known to Sonja, and they started spending time together.

When I returned, the truth came out. Sonja admitted to having stolen "my" boyfriend. We talked about it—amazingly enough, without a lot of emotionalism or drama—and decided that no boy was worth jeopardizing our friendship. Sonja dialed his number, I picked up another receiver, and together we made a "Dear John" call. As cute as he was, our friendship was way more important.

When I look back at the depth and quality of our relationship, I am simply amazed. I know I must have driven Sonja crazy at times. Walking to school with me every day meant earning at least a dozen late slips a year, for which she was not to blame. I was the flighty extrovert; she was the voice of reason. I had the wild imagination; she, the dry sense of humor. Outside my family, no one but Sonja could have known how fragile I truly was. How often she protected me, comforted me, and steadied me! Without her, this social butterfly would have dissolved like tissue paper in a pounding rain.

At my wedding reception, when I introduced Sonja with those lyrics from "Seasons in the Sun," I didn't quote the line that came next. Now, it haunts me, because it's basically a farewell to a dying friend.

During the summer months before Sonja's return to Calgary, I had been studying the life of King David and was deeply touched by the biblical account of his final encounter with his best friend, Jonathan, who knew that he was about to die. In a moving scene of love, grief, loyalty, and commitment, Jonathan asked David to make a solemn promise: that when the battle was over and the dust had settled on his grave, David would take care of his family.

On Tuesday, September 19, I was on my way to see Sonja with the intention of making a similar promise to her. I knew her fragile body was failing fast, and I struggled to prepare myself emotionally for what I knew might be our last encounter this side of heaven. I stood in the main lobby of the Foothills Hospital, waiting for one of the six elevators to admit me. One set of doors opened, and out stepped Sonja's mom, Bonnie, and her sister Paula. They were as surprised to see me as I was to see them, and we stood there, looking at each other, not sure what to say in such a heavy moment.

Finally, Paula broke the silence. "She's gone!"

I stood there silently, trying to take it in.

I had missed my chance to say good-bye by mere moments.

Paula broke the silence. "She's gone!" I had missed my chance to say good-bye by mere moments.

Thankfully, I had been to see Sonja a few days prior. I had helped her into a wheelchair and moved her outside into the sunshine. She'd always loved the sun. We'd talked and prayed together. I'd hugged her and told her I loved her. But there was so much more to say.

I had tried to see Sonja two more times before she passed away, but neither occasion was convenient; either the room had been full of relatives or doctors, or Sonja had been taken elsewhere for tests. We never got to say all there was to say—to laugh at all our old jokes, to smile at all our long-held secrets, to relive all our precious memories. I wish I'd had the maturity when we were teenagers, or the sensitivity later, when the miles came between us, to tell her just how much she had always meant to me.

Losing Sonja was like having the core of my childhood ripped out of me. That sensitive, silly young girl still living somewhere deep inside of me feels such a profound sense of loss.

Yet, in other ways, I have not lost Sonja at all. I would not be who I am today if it hadn't been for her. I would not enjoy the rapport I do with other women. The close connection I had with Sonja has become the standard, the template, for every friendship I've formed since knowing her—the foundation of empathy and trust on which all of my relationships have been built.

Thank you, Sonja, my friend.

JUST ONE FRIEND

Questions for Reflection and Discussion

1. Who were your closest friends in childhood and throughout adolescence? What was the basis for these friendships? (In other words, what common ground did you share?)

2. Were any of your childhood friendships similar to Donna's deep friendship with Sonja? How so? How were they different?

3. What role did your earliest friendships play in establishing the foundation for future relationships in your life?

4. If you had the opportunity to express your appreciation to your closest childhood friend, what would you say?

5. What's stopping you?

2

EVERYONE NEEDS A FRIEND

When my thoughts turn to friendship, two things amaze me. The first is the quantity and quality of friendships I have enjoyed. Perhaps it was the experience of having one true, close friend in my formative years that prepared me to make friends easily later on in life.

The second thing that amazes me when I think about friendship is how few women can say the same thing—that they've had a host of deep, meaningful friendships. In my travels and various speaking engagements on relationship—especially those that focus on friendship, in particular—I am continually reminded of how many women are lonely and desperate for community with other women. The question I hear most often is, "How can I find a true friend?"

Even so, I struggle for a response every time. One reason is that it's difficult for me to identify with that problem. Most women would feel incredibly grateful to have just one friend like Sonja—one deeply satisfying connection—and yet I have been blessed by a multitude of such friendships, certainly more than my fair share. Why do so many women go through life never enjoying the closeness, the safety, the comfort found in a relationship with a true friend?

Stumbling Blocks to Satisfying Friendship

A lack of satisfying friendships often revolves around our emotional health. Some women are particularly fearful of letting themselves be truly known. Others avoid relationships because they are afraid of rejection and abandonment. Still others are crippled by comparison, either feeling inferior or superior to the women they might otherwise have befriended. And the majority are simply too busy to put in the time it takes to cultivate a deep friendship. These issues and others prevent many women from taking the risk of allowing other women to walk into their lives and leave footprints on their hearts.

> If we insist on wearing a mask and playing a part before the world, we will never experience the joy of unqualified acceptance.

Of all the barriers to genuine friendship, the biggest is probably the reluctance to take off our masks—the fear of being known, because of the possibility of our being found wanting. If we insist on wearing a mask and playing a part before the world, rather than letting our guard down and being vulnerable, we will never experience the joy of unqualified acceptance.

The Risks of Being Known

Years ago, I read a story that captures—in a humorous way—the risks of being known. A pastor and his wife were expecting company for dessert one evening. The pastor had come home late from work, delaying dinner—and leaving his wife with little time to tidy up before her guests arrived. She was rushing around the kitchen, trying to clean up, when—alas!—the guests showed up ahead of schedule. As they were pulling into the driveway, she had a brilliant idea. She hastily piled all of the dirty dinner dishes and utensils on a baking sheet and slid it into the oven, out of sight. It was a miracle—in under thirty seconds, the formerly messy kitchen was spotless, and the woman was able to greet her guests at the door with a smile.

About an hour into the visit, the pastor's wife excused herself and went to the kitchen to prepare the dessert.

One of her guests stood up and followed her. "Let me help you," she said.

The hostess breathed a sigh of relief that the dirty dishes were safely stashed away. Her kitchen would pass a white-glove inspection, as long as no one opened the oven.

"What a wonderful kitchen this is," her guest remarked, gazing about the room. "We're thinking of remodeling ours, and I love to see what other people have done." Walking across the kitchen, she declared, "What a nice, big oven!" And she proceeded to open the door, at which point the pile of dishes shifted, and all of them came spilling out at her feet.

The two women stood there in stunned silence. The pastor's wife tried to think of something to say—some way to explain her odd housekeeping methods—but all she could think of was, "Don't worry; I keep all the dessert dishes over here in the cabinet."

How we like to present to the world a version of ourselves that would never stand for dirty dishes in the kitchen. Imagine my saying, "That's right—we don't get dishes dirty in the Carter household; that would be so unsanitary! We've taught the children to eat in such a way that no crumbs are left on their plates." The reality is, it looks as if the goal is to skip the plate and get the crumbs straight on the carpet—at the very beginning of the meal! When we clear the table after dinner, four perfect disks, like crop circles of cleanliness, mark the areas where the plates had been.

Yet many of us insist on pretending that we've never made a mess in our lives. We're never selfish or petty; we never yell at our kids, nor do we have to; there are no skeletons in our closets or under our beds—or dust bunnies, for that matter.

Churchgoing women can be the worst when it comes to perpetuating this fictitious front. Somehow, we've come to believe that admitting we have problems puts a blemish on our reputation as Christians. This belief is completely erroneous, and yet it worms its way into our minds, often through painful personal experiences.

My husband and I entered our second church ministry with the youthful optimism of Confederate privates at the first battle of the Civil War. Six years later, the final two of which seemed to me like a slow, agonizing death, we left that church, feeling like those same privates the day General Robert E. Lee surrendered at Appomattox. All of our youthful naiveté, idealism, and energy had been bled dry onto the battlefield; we were broken and exhausted.

Mustering any and all of the fight left in us, we struggled to keep our hearts right. I did not want to become embittered, like some of the pastors' wives I had come across during our first decade of ministry. But I discovered that forgiveness and healing are more like a journey than a single, onetime event. They are a path you choose to walk until you come to the end, and you know it's the end only when you've reached it, never before.

> Forgiveness and healing are a path you choose to walk until you come to the end, and you know it's the end only when you've reached it, never before.

At one point along this journey, I took a risk and shared my pain with an older woman in another church. She responded, in a condescending tone, "You sound a little bitter, dear."

She was right. I *was* bitter. But I desperately needed a friend to love and accept me in my pain and help me find the way out of my self-made maze of resentment. What I got instead was a polite rebuke that felt like iodine poured into an open wound. The implication of that woman's statement was that I was "bad" to have gotten to this place of bitterness. I was "bad" to be angry; "bad" because I should have gotten over it by now.

It is never fun to make yourself vulnerable with someone you thought was safe, only to be offered some pat, patronizing answer that compounds your feelings of guilt and shame rather than relieves them.

Friendship and the Fall

God created us for relationship. He desired friendship with His created beings. But He also endowed us with free will—the ability to choose a relationship with Him. He didn't want us to be like robots or slaves, programmed or required to serve Him. He wanted our love, freely given.

God had the perfect relationship with the first created man, Adam. Yet He recognized Adam's need for someone like himself with whom to be in relationship.

> *Then the Lord God said, "It is not good for the man to be alone. I will make a helper who is just right for him."*
> (Genesis 2:18)

Enter: Eve.

Adam and Eve lived in perfect contentment, finding their every need met in relationship with God and with each other. There was never a misunderstanding, never a communication problem, no unmet expectations, no jealousy—no breakdown of relationship whatsoever. Eve instinctively knew which direction to hang the toilet paper roll, and Adam never forgot to put the toilet seat down after he was done.

This is no small thing. My husband and I had to learn some of these basic bylaws of matrimony. My husband didn't know that there are pink jobs and blue jobs, and that taking out the garbage is *definitely* a blue job. Believe it or not, he didn't realize that when you make up a bed with floral sheets, the flowers must "grow" upward toward the pillows.

I had some learning of my own to do. I'd never known there was a proper way to fold socks. I had always believed that as long as the matching socks stayed attached in the drawer, it was all good. Not true, I soon discovered. The toes of the socks must never flop about willy-nilly but must remain tucked inside the cuff of the enfolding outer sock.

Silly me. I had so much to learn. But not Eve and her man. Everything was literally perfect between them until they decided to exercise their ability to choose whether or not to obey the one and only restriction God had placed on them.

This event ushered sin into the world, and nothing has been the same since. The effect of sin was separation, both from God and from one another. The first example was the intentional separation that occurred when Adam and Eve hid from God out of fear. (See Genesis 3:8–10.) Consequently, Adam and Eve were banished from their terrestrial paradise, and they brought upon themselves the curse of sin, which is physical and relational death—a curse that is automatically inherited by all of their descendants. Yet we will explore, as we continue on this journey together, how God made a way for human beings to remain in fellowship with Him, both on earth and for eternity, by sending His Son to break the curse.

Sometimes, when our most satisfying relationships are at their best—in rare moments of intimacy that punctuate the ordinary days of our friendships—we get a glimpse of the kind of relationship God intended for us to enjoy with one another. In general, however, even the happiest marriages and closest friendships are hard work. At times, they can even be a nightmare.

> Even though we may get hurt, and even though we may hurt others, those hurts are well worth the emotional sustenance our relationships provide.

Yet our need for human relationship remains. Even though we may get hurt, and even though we may hurt others, those hurts are well worth the emotional sustenance our relationships provide. And you can be sure that the pain of friendlessness—of loneliness, abandonment, and disconnectedness—is far worse. Unless we establish a network of friends with whom we feel comfortable being authentic, we are guaranteed to suffer.

The Beauty of Bonding

The labor and delivery that concluded my first pregnancy were prolonged and painful for everyone involved. For me, mostly. My husband likes to joke that he had to take a week off of work to be my labor coach. Eventually, however—with the help of a small army of medical professionals and the infamous "salad spoons," I gave birth to a tiny baby girl, whom we named Kendall Hope.

Truthfully, I had spent considerable time during my pregnancy worrying that I might not be maternal enough. I mean, I had always seen myself more as the career type. But, seven years into my marriage, I finally realized the futility of trying to raise my husband. It seemed like it was time to have children, while I still had a few good child-bearing years left.

When the pushing and panting were finally over, I was exhausted but relieved. I nursed my baby for a few minutes, before they strapped a lump of ice to my poor, bruised undercarriage, gave me a sleeping pill, and…in truth, I don't remember anything after that.

I do remember waking up the next morning and feeling quite amazed that I had gone through a complicated childbirth and survived. I was still hooked up to all kinds of IV tubes and equipment, and I didn't even ask to see my baby. Eventually, they brought her to me, this little stranger, and I spent the day learning to care for her.

As I held, changed, nursed, and cuddled my little girl that day, something happened—something magical that I was totally unprepared for. A tidal wave of emotion swept over me—a love so powerful for that little one. I had never felt anything like it. The mysterious, intimate connection that the psychologists call "bonding" was happening between us, mother and daughter.

I wanted to be with my baby, and she wanted to be with me. She instinctively knew my voice. Within hours of her birth, I could distinguish her cry from that of every other infant in the hospital. When the nurse came to my room to take Kendall to the nursery for the night, I cried. I could hardly bear to be separated from this small person who, just that morning, had been a stranger to me.

That is bonding. That sense of intimate connectedness, of wanting to be together, of desiring to give and receive from one another; of feeling safe and content in each other's presence; of truly knowing and truly being known.

Hindrances to Bonding

Sadly, the only bonding many women will know occurs when they give birth; they don't experience that joyful intimacy with a fellow adult. In this broken, sin-scarred world, some people live a lifetime and never experience even one true, intimate relationship. An emotional wound sustained early in childhood may cause a once open, vulnerable person to go into hiding for years—even for the rest of her life. And a person in hiding can't bond with anyone. The price of protecting her heart is utter isolation.

> A person in hiding can't bond with anyone.

A friend of mine experienced a period of self-imposed exile like I've just described, and he vividly remembers how it began. As a little boy, he went to work with his father one Saturday. He felt proud and privileged to be participating in such an important mission with his daddy. Overwhelmed with emotion as the two of them walked hand in hand along the sidewalk downtown, the boy felt his feelings bubble to the surface, and he gave them a voice. "I love you, Dad," he said, with childlike sincerity.

The only sound that followed his heartfelt declaration was the sound of their footsteps, one after the other. Without breaking stride or making eye contact, the boy's father finally said, "That's nice." In that instant, a heart was wounded, an innocence was lost, and a vow was made. *I'll never do that again*, the boy said to himself. *It isn't good to open your heart. It hurts to offer your love. It may not be accepted and returned. It's not worth the risk. I won't say those words again.* And, for many years, he kept his word.

Some people who have been badly wounded by someone they trusted go so long without taking the risk of being vulnerable that they forget how to bond. Or, they carry a secret—a feeling of shame, and, with that shame, the certainty that if others knew the truth about them, they would reject them. Such individuals believe that the hidden realities of their past or inner lives are so much worse than the realities that lie below the surface of the lives of other people.

They may reach the conclusion that knowing others, and truly being known by others, is not worth the risk of potential pain. It seems easier to ignore that persistent yearning for intimacy than to face exposure and possible rejection. Eventually, the yearning subsides into a dull ache that stops demanding their attention, but it doesn't go away. Like an undiagnosed infection, it slowly invades their emotional lives. While their hearts are becoming atrophied, they may be thinking, *I'm getting along just fine on my own. I don't need anybody.*

A Biblical Picture of Bonding

God wants so much more for us. He wants us to be joined together, like the parts of a body. The apostle Paul expressed it like this: *"We are joined together in his body by his strong sinews, and we grow only as we get our nourishment and strength from God"* (Colossians 2:19).

In the Bible, the church universal is described as the body of Christ, with Christ Himself as the Head.

The human body has many parts, but the many parts make up only one body. So it is with the body of Christ....Yes, the body has many different parts, not just one part. If the foot says, "I am not a part of the body because I am not a hand," that does not make it any less a part of the body. And if the ear says, "I am not part of the body because I am only an ear and not an eye," would that make it any less a part of the body? Suppose the whole body were an eye—then how would you hear? Or if your whole body were just one big ear, how could you smell anything? But God made our bodies with many parts, and he has put each part just where he wants it. What a strange thing a body would be if it had only one part! Yes, there are many parts, but only one body. The eye can never say to the hand, "I don't need you." The head can't say to the feet, "I don't need you."

(1 Corinthians 12:12, 14–21)

Whoever heard of a body part getting along without the rest of the body? (I'm not talking about the efforts of stem-cell researchers to grow livers, lungs, and other organs in Petri dishes.) We need each other, just as our individual body parts need each other—collectively, as a body—to function. And we can be to one another what we are meant to be only when we come out from behind our walls of self-seclusion and form connections that are intimate and authentic.

I know a woman named Terri who was involved in a very serious car accident when she was a teenager. At the hospital, the doctors examined her arm, which was badly mangled, and decided that amputation was the only viable solution. Even if the shattered bone could be mended, there just wasn't enough skin and muscle left to hold the arm together. But then, one surgeon had a brilliant idea. He suggested that they sew what was left of her arm to her abdomen. The thought was that, being connected to an adequate blood supply, Terri's arm would generate enough new tissue that it could eventually be detached safely from her abdomen. This arm would never look the same as her other arm, but if her nerves survived, Terri would at least have partial use of her hand. Amazingly, the procedure worked.

What a graphic picture! We were created for relationship. And God shows us through the image of the body that we need each other. An arm that is partially torn away from the shoulder, as Terri's was, will gradually decompose from gangrene. Only by connection to the body may it heal and grow.

God created us for relationship, with Him and with one another, in spite of the risks involved—from exposure and rejection to arguments and bruised egos. It is only in community with Christ and His people that we receive the love, acceptance, emotional healing, safety, nurture, and comfort we need to be all Jesus intends us to be.

How do we move from a place of self-protective hiding into the openness of genuine community? How can a person break both the walls and the vows that have built a fortress around her heart? Only by taking another risk. By deciding that the only thing worse than the intense pain of being known and rejected is the certainty of the low-grade, long-term pain of never being known by anyone at all.

Perhaps you have acknowledged your need for relationships, and now the question on your heart is this: "How can I find a true friend who can be trusted with my unmasked self?" To discover the answer to this question, you have to know what you're looking for. I'd like to be your guide in this process of discovery.

EVERYONE NEEDS A FRIEND

Questions for Reflection and Discussion

1. Have you struggled at some point in your life (or perhaps your whole life) to establish satisfying friendships? If so, what are the explanations you have offered yourself to justify this struggle?

2. How has the fear of being known and possibly rejected played out in your life? Can you think of situations when you deliberately backed away from a friend just when she was beginning to see the real you?

3. Can you think of a time when you attempted to mislead others into thinking you were more together than you really were?

4. Have you ever taken the risk of sharing some private emotion, wound, or struggle with someone you thought was safe, only to have your trust betrayed somehow? If so, how has this experience affected your ability to bond with others?

5. What are your thoughts on the metaphor of the body of Christ, as expressed by Paul in Colossians 2:19? Here is the verse again, for a refresher: *"We are joined together in his body by his strong sinews, and we grow only as we get our nourishment and strength from God."*

6. Are you ready to take the risk of trusting again? If not, what is holding you back?

Part II

THE PORTRAIT OF FRIENDSHIP

3

BEING THERE

If I were to compare the profiles of all of my face-to-face friends, I would revel in their diversity. I would recall touching stories, humorous moments, and particular words and phrases unique to each individual. But I would also be struck by their similarities. You see, each of these profiles represents a friendship in which eight characteristics are woven, in varying degrees, into the very fabric of the relationship. And they are present wherever true friendship is found. These eight qualities are:

+ Affinity

+ Availability

+ Authenticity

+ Ability to be at ease

+ Affirmation

+ Acceptance
+ Accountability
+ Assistance

In this chapter and the three that follow it, we will examine these traits "up close and personal." Let's start with affinity.

Affinity

Growing up, I always thought I would marry a man who was the strong, silent type. It seems that couples tend to consist of an extrovert and an introvert. Because I have always been outgoing, I figured I was supposed to end up with someone who was more quiet and reserved. After all, opposites attract, right?

To say that my husband is not an introvert would be the understatement of the ages. Randy is the kind of guy who laughs so loudly at a funny movie, everyone else in the theater looks around to see who's making all the noise.

When our kids were little, their friends were afraid of Randy because he is so big and so loud. He'd burst in through the door, see Kendall and her little friend, and roar, "Hi, girlies!" Our daughter's smile would quickly morph into a study in confusion and concern when her cowering friend burst into tears. Kendall didn't get it. She knew her daddy was safe. She'd been listening to that booming voice since she was in the womb. Randy would speak to her through my navel as if it was a microphone—not that he's ever needed one.

Randy really has a heart for children, and their fear of him always caused him grief. (It should be stated that he didn't mind nearly as much when, later on, our daughters' boyfriends also found him intimidating.) Yet he can't help but be loud, even when he's being tender. My friend Patty described him well when she said, "Randy just really fills up the room."

I'm thankful I didn't marry the strong, silent type. If I had, I would have missed out on the stimulating relationship I have with my fun-loving husband. And if I had been determined to seek out a quiet kind of man, I never would have known the excitement of the sparks that fly when two extroverts cohabitate.

> Whether we're seeking a spouse or a new friend, we shouldn't allow stereotypes and preconceived notions to limit our search.

Whether we're seeking a spouse or a new friend, we shouldn't allow stereotypes and preconceived notions to limit our search. If we do, we may miss out on a relationship with someone who would have enriched our life, whether through our differences or similarities.

Affinity by Accident

I have always been a city girl. I just didn't know how much until we moved to a small town in British Columbia's Fraser Valley. They called it a city—a stretch, in my opinion, considering the lack of any buildings over five stories high.

Apparently everyone who lived there knew the difference between a cow and a heifer. How I had managed to stumble through some thirty years of existence without picking up such critical knowledge escapes me. Given the reactions I got when I asked what the difference was, you would have thought I was inquiring about the difference between a dinosaur and a doughnut.

We're talking rural. And stable. Those who were born and raised there tended to stay, get married, start a family, and remain until their dying day. Change didn't come easily at all.

I was accustomed to a very different way of life, and I wondered if I would ever find a friend in this place that seemed so foreign.

One day, I snapped. The spirit of the Fraser Valley came over me, and I woke up one morning determined to make dill pickles. I had never canned anything in my life, but there, in the valley, it's just what you do. I won't bore you with all the details of what came to be known in our family as "killer dills," but I will say that it was a "wake up and smell the vinegar" kind of day.

When my husband came home from work that evening, I told him, "Hon, you've got to get me out of here—fast. I've started canning and I can't stop. It could be quilting next, or… or…crafts!"

Now, don't get me wrong—I know many warm, wonderful, intelligent women who quilt, can vegetables, and create all sorts of crafts. But it is *so* not like me to do any of those things. Finding another woman with whom I shared an immediate affinity proved very difficult in the land of gifted homemaking.

> The quality of our relationships is based, to a degree, on the quality of what has drawn us together.

The dictionary defines *affinity* as "a natural liking, taste, or inclination towards a person or thing." Two people with an affinity are drawn to each other, for various reasons. Affinities often arise among individuals with shared interests, common causes, or like-minded ways of thinking. And the quality of our relationships is based, to a degree, on the quality of what has drawn us together—our affinity. For example, a friendship that is based on a mutual passion for shoe shopping may be a lot of fun, but a friendship that's based on something deeper, within our souls, is a real treasure.

Finally, I found her, right there in the valley—another woman who didn't quilt or can or make crafts. A woman who has been known, in fact, to hem clothes with a stapler. A woman who loves to shop for shoes *and* who lies awake at night trying to figure out how to mentor other women more effectively. Someone who loves to read, to learn, to grow, and to lead. My kind of woman.

Patty and I discovered our affinity by accident. It seemed we were the only two women in our church who thought that "because we've always done it that way" wasn't a good enough reason to continue doing something a certain way.

Several more seasoned leaders involved in women's ministry at our church asked us to put our heads together and redesign the program. The crazy thing is, we thought they were serious. We began to brainstorm how we could reach women more effectively as a church group. As we talked and dreamed together, we experienced such unity. It was as if each of us had been wandering around with half of the pieces to the same jigsaw puzzle. Once we figured out how they all fit together, it was more exhilarating than words can say.

Here we were, two women whose backgrounds were so different that we might as well have been born in different centuries on different continents. But when it came to our concern for the women of our church and community, our priorities were aligned and our hearts were synchronized.

With a great deal of excitement, we revealed our plans to the women's ministry leaders. To conclude our presentation, we unveiled the new logo we had designed, which featured the new name we'd chosen for the program.

The women looked at us like we had just kicked the United States out of NATO. They didn't get it. They didn't get us. I think they hated everything in our presentation, except for maybe the new logo.

We were frustrated that day, but we weren't devastated. We had learned something about affinity. It doesn't have to do with where you were raised—whether in the city or the country—your family background, or even your age. At the seminal level, it has everything to do with passion—what makes you weep or pound your fists on the table or lie awake at night, too excited to sleep.

Two other things became clear to Patty and me through that experience. First, we knew that we were going to be friends for life. Second, we realized that we would never be content to settle for the status quo in ministry. Our greatest passion was helping women grow in their faith, and we were ready to use whatever means necessary—including drastic change—to stay relevant to the women we were trying to reach. And so, a ministry partnership was launched—one that is ever deepening with each passing year.

For years, Patty and I have traveled all over Canada together, speaking to women and fulfilling our mutual passion—the passion to see women make meaningful connections with each other and with God. What a rush we get from watching other women be transformed by the power of God! And how sweet to share these experiences with my wonderful, passionate, shoe-crazy, stapler-brandishing friend!

Recognizing Affinity

How do you know when you share an affinity with someone? Finding a depth of commonality with another person usually requires some investigation. In many cases, though, we don't even have to think about it; we simply "click" through instant attraction. Other times, it takes a little longer to plumb beneath the surface to uncover the passions that lie closer to the heart. Discovering shared passions can be as uncomplicated as learning to ask open-ended questions, such as: "What are you reading these days?" "How do you prefer to spend your free time?" "What kinds of films really move you?"

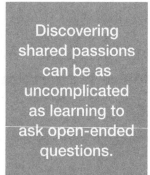

Discovering shared passions can be as uncomplicated as learning to ask open-ended questions.

When you take the risk of revealing your personal values, interests, and priorities, as well as probing to know someone else's, you'll quickly determine what, if any, common ground you share. Your relationship may start out as a pursuit of mutual interests you discover right away (such as shoe shopping) and then go deeper (such as volunteering together) as you come to know and trust each other. Relationships like this offer a safe place where we are accepted, cherished, and challenged to become all that we can be.

Finding affinity with someone is what makes diving into the friendship a pleasure rather than a duty. If you are blessed enough to experience the "click" early on, be sure to act on it right away. Schedule time together and see if the connection grows as you get to know one another better. If there is no immediate "click," but you feel the potential for affinity is there, take the risk of exploring the possibility and be attentive for a confirming echo from the other side. When your newfound affinity confirms the friendship is worth the investment of your time, that is an invitation to employ the quality of availability.

Availability

"I'm here for you." This phrase is often heard but seldom translated into action. What a rare and precious gift is the presence of a friend who is always there, steadfastly standing by through the ups and downs of life: times of elation, grief, rage, and confusion.

Romans 12:15 captures the essence of an available friend: *"When others are happy, be happy with them. If they are sad, share their sorrow."* It is a terrible disappointment to be let down by a friend who promised to be there but wasn't. And it is an unexpected comfort to enjoy the presence of one who never said the words but showed up, just the same.

Only days before Sonja went to be with Jesus, she and Brian planned her memorial service. She wanted me to sing but told Brian she wasn't sure I'd be able to. Her reasoning was sound. Since I'm moved to tears by everything from Disney movies to ribbon-cutting ceremonies, there was little hope that I could bear up while singing at the farewell service of my oldest friend. I wasn't sure I could do it, either, but one thing I knew: if Sonja wanted me to sing, I was going to give it my best effort.

I asked several friends to pray for me. And they must have, because even though I cried buckets that day, I was able to sing the song Sonja and Brian had requested with an appropriate balance of emotion and control.

But one of my friends went above and beyond what I'd asked. She took off work on a busy afternoon to come to the funeral and sit at the back of the auditorium during a service for a woman she'd never met, just to offer nods of encouragement as she prayed me through a very difficult hour.

Sometimes, being a good friend is as simple as being there, making yourself available. You may have the most winsome personality in the world. You may be the type of person who lights up a room just by walking in. But if you are not there for your friends when it counts, you lack the key trait of availability.

Sometimes, being a good friend is as simple as making yourself available.

Of course, no friend, no matter how committed, can be present all the time. But being available means being willing to be inconvenienced. It means being committed to spending time with someone, despite your busy schedule. It means saying, "If you need me, you can call anytime, 24/7, and I will drop everything and come." A really great friend is so in tune with her friends and loved ones that she senses when she is needed most, even when those people lack the ability or the willpower to call for help.

The Difference a Simple Phone Call Can Make

Early in his itinerant speaking ministry, my husband, Randy, was still learning the limits of his physical and emotional endurance. He often overscheduled himself and would end up feeling profoundly depleted from intense seasons of ministry. I was always amazed by how quickly he bounced back. One time, however, he just didn't have the strength. Even after several weeks of downtime, he hadn't recovered from a summer spent speaking at youth camps. Living on adrenaline for an extended period of time had depleted his energy account, and he began to experience symptoms of the result: burnout.

I was scared, quite frankly. I wanted him to feel better, to behave normally. I tried encouraging him to take a proactive approach—to "get over it." Of course, I didn't know then what I know now: that we were dealing with burnout-induced depression, and that being proactive is not really an option for those battling true depression. In these times, they lack the emotional and physical energy to initiate anything.

But this was uncharted territory for Randy and me. Neither of us understood what was going on. I kept saying to him, "Why don't you call your friend Les?" Spending time with Les had proven almost therapeutic for him in the past. The two of them usually did something involving noise, speed, and smoke, and Randy always came home a new man.

But he wouldn't pick up the phone. I thought of calling Les myself, but I didn't have to. While I prayed and waited, Les called Randy.

The call probably went something like this:

Les: "Hey buddy, how are ya?"

Randy: Long pause, followed by a ragged breath.

Les: "Buddy, what's wrong?"

Randy: "I don't know."

Les: "I'm coming to get you tomorrow. We're going for coffee."

Just like that, a busy man with an important job turned his schedule upside down and rushed to the side of his friend. That's availability.

Follow Through on Your Offers to Help

It's one thing to say to a friend, "If there's anything I can do, just call." It's something else altogether to look for a way to lift the load and just do it. The people who need us the most often feel extremely reluctant to ask for help, to place themselves in a position of admitting a need, to impose on our busy schedules.

To realize the truth of this, we have only to think of the last time we needed someone. We were probably sure that our need wasn't big enough, that our resources weren't depleted enough, and that we weren't worthy enough. The reality is that all of us are needy, in varying degrees, at one time or another. But a friend who is available doesn't care where your need ranks on the Richter scale that measures the crises of life. She doesn't care whether you should be able to pull yourself up by your own bootstraps. All she cares about is bringing comfort and companionship to a heart that's lonely, despairing, or overwhelmed.

Several weeks ago, I received some bad news concerning my precious sister's health. I was devastated. I felt sad, debilitated, and exhausted. Even now, the gravity of the situation often overwhelms me. I deeply appreciate the friends who have been there for me in various ways. One woman named Sandie, with whom I have a growing friendship that is not yet close, went above and beyond the usual "Let me know if there's anything I can do." She said, "I want to help. I can cook and bake, walk your dog, run errands, and buy groceries. I can clean, pick up dry cleaning, or do laundry. What would be the most helpful?" Wow! Even though I don't know Sandie really well, I could tell that her offer wasn't hollow, like a chocolate Easter bunny. This proposal was solid chocolate. She really wanted to help.

Wendy, who is the executive director of a high-energy organization and sits on more than one influential board, treated me to dinner at a lovely restaurant. During the course of the meal, she looked me in the eye and said, "If you need me, call. I may not be able to come immediately, but within twenty-four hours, I will be there." She also offered to take on any speaking engagements I might feel unable to fulfill. I knew she meant it.

Still another close friend, Becky, responded to my e-mails of prayer requests not just promising to pray for me but actually typing out her prayers as a reply message and sending them to me. As I read her beautiful, thoughtful words, I was assured that someone was praying for me—someone who truly understood the enormity of the situation I faced and how I felt about it.

These examples are to show the simple ways in which you can make yourself available to someone who needs you. All it takes is caring enough and keeping in touch, so that you'll know when that is.

The Gift of Presence

I was so excited over my second pregnancy. We had planned it so that our children would be three years apart—close enough to share some common interests, but not so close as to wear us out in the early years. And we wanted two kids—only two—or, as my husband pointed out, we would have to go from a man-on-man to a zone parental defense strategy.

Everything was going according to plan until I began to bleed. I didn't panic at first, because there was no cramping, and I had spotted a couple of times during my first pregnancy. But when the bleeding continued for days, I became concerned. I remembered the doctor saying he believed my dates were off because my "bump" had seemed a bit small. It seemed highly possible that I would lose my child.

For days, I hovered in the uncertain emotional airspace between hope and grief. I desperately wanted this baby. Now, in the second trimester, I was showing, and word was getting out that I was pregnant. That week, it seemed that everywhere I went, someone congratulated me on my "wonderful news." I kept thinking, *If only you knew the emotional roller coaster I'm on right now.*

To add to my emotional instability, my husband had to attend a speaking engagement outside the country. It had been booked for many months, and so it wasn't the kind of thing you could just cancel. He hated to leave me, but I insisted that he keep his commitment.

The day he left, I made a doctor's appointment. I had bled for ten days without a miscarriage, and I needed to know whether the child I was carrying was living or dead. My sister Debbie called me and asked, "Who's going to the doctor with you?" I responded, "No one." I somehow felt that being adult meant having to deal with this sort of issue alone.

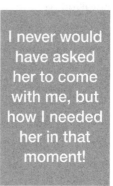

I never would have asked her to come with me, but how I needed her in that moment!

I never would have asked her to come with me, but she did, and I was so grateful. A pelvic exam revealed no trace of life pulsating inside my womb. The pain of loss pushed itself up into a lump in my throat. I came out of the examining room and walked straight into my sister's arms, where, enveloped by that comfort, I sobbed in grief and disappointment. How I needed her in that moment!

If she had considered herself too busy to insist on coming with me, I would have survived. I would have spared all of the curious onlookers in the waiting room and discreetly saved my tears for the drive home. But I would not have experienced the comfort of her presence—the comfort of sharing my grief with someone who loved me enough to be there for me.

As the months passed, I dreaded the approach of my former due date. The day arrived, once so eagerly anticipated, now soaked in disappointment and loss. But I was not alone in my sadness. Debbie remembered me and sent a bouquet of flowers. She remembered because she had been there for me. Through her gift of remembrance, I knew that she still was there for me.

Never do we feel lonelier than when we have news to share, whether joyful or painful, and no one to share it with. Solo celebrations are just as painful as having to bear a great grief all alone. In the company of a beloved friend, a smile becomes a celebration. A companion in life's valleys can keep us from the edge of despair. And the company of a friend on the mundane plateaus just makes life more interesting. The quality of availability is what enables us to infuse our friendships with all the other necessary traits, as we will see in the pages ahead.

BEING THERE

Questions for Reflection and Discussion

1. Have you ever befriended someone who initially did not seem "your type"? Describe your most prominent differences and then discuss why the friendship works anyway.

2. What are your primary passions in life, whether "shallow" (like shoe shopping) or profound (like stopping human trafficking)? Do you have friends who share those same passions?

3. Why and how do shared passions draw us to others?

4. Who has been there for you when it has counted?

5. Has there been a time when you looked for someone with whom to share a trial or a triumph, but no one was there to

meet that need? Share or reflect on that experience. What were you really looking for in that moment?

6. How can we be tuned in enough to the needs of our closest friends so that we may be prepared to go to them when they lack the ability to ask for help?

7. Romans 12:15 says, *"When others are happy, be happy with them. If they are sad, share their sorrow."* Try to think of some practical ways in which you could live out this verse in your relationships.

4

THE BLONDE
LEADING THE BLONDE

How are you?"

"Great, just great."

"Really? Are you telling the truth? Well, it doesn't really matter, because I actually wasn't listening for your answer. In any event, I've already traveled five feet out of earshot."

We may not be so blunt, but if we voiced our thoughts, they'd sound a lot like that, wouldn't they? Most of the time, the question "How are you?" elicits an insincere response—and it's often posed with equal insincerity.

When I was a young adult, I decided to do a little experiment for a short while. I tried being authentic whenever someone asked me how I was. And I quickly discovered that it's a major social faux pas to respond truthfully if you're not

"Great, just great!" Most people really don't want to know. If someone honestly cares about how you are doing, she words the question some other way.

The socially correct response to the query "How are you?" is "Fine." In most cases, the word *fine* is an acronym that means "feelings inside not expressed."

Authenticity

An authentic friendship is one in which it's safe to say, "I'm not fine; in fact, I'm really lousy." And that honesty is received with compassion and concern.

I am involved with a small group of women who call themselves the Chicks' Boys Club. The name was chosen because some of the members disliked the stereotypes associated with women's groups. The consensus was that a "boys club" would be far more fun. And, given how much we laugh and carry on together, it's hard to imagine another boys club being any more enjoyable than ours! We also pray together and share from the heart. In fact, every time we meet, we take turns answering this question: "How is your heart?"

Sometimes, most of us are "Just great." Usually, though, at least one or more of us is struggling. On occasion, someone will even say, "Pass," which the rest of us translate like this: "I need you to pray for me, but I can't say more because I have to go to work after this and I don't want to cry so much that my mascara runs off." Whether our response is "Great," "Struggling," or "Pass," none of us is ever "Fine." We don't have to pretend. We understand the importance of acknowledging our problems if we're going to solve them; of owning our wounds if they're going to heal. Pretending to be fine won't make our wounds go away;

it only makes us feel lonelier and further convinces us that we are the only ones who have struggled with this issue, this problem, this pain.

When we trust someone enough to be authentic and vulnerable with her, we are freed to share our feelings and to accept her wisdom and comfort. It also gives her the assurance that she can trust us with her feelings and count on us to offer consolation in times of turbulence.

When Authenticity Is Uncomfortable

How do we get to the place of trusting one friend, let alone a group of friends, with our innermost thoughts, emotions, and struggles? How can we practice authenticity without feeling uncomfortable and self-conscious? The process is gradual, for trust must be earned over time. True authenticity in a relationship must be both gradual and reciprocal.

Yet, even when we proceed with caution, trusting someone else with our true self is dangerous and difficult. There are many risks involved, to be sure. Whenever we place our trust in someone else, she may reward us with warm acceptance, but it's also possible that she will betray our confidence. One thing is certain: if we never take the risk of beginning to trust someone, we will never know the satisfaction of deeply authentic relationships, the most fulfilling of which require a lifetime to build.

> If we never take the risk of beginning to trust someone, we will never know the satisfaction of deeply authentic relationships, the most fulfilling of which require a lifetime to build.

A friendship with someone who will guard our secrets as her own may take years to develop. But the effort is worth it when you consider the reward of having a fellow human being who treasures the privilege of knowing a part of us that few others ever see and is willing to be equally open with us, in return. You may begin by saying, "May I share something personal with you? I'm not really comfortable sharing my innermost thoughts, but I want you to know the real me, and this issue is really weighing on me now." The hearer of that vulnerable statement then thinks to herself, *What I'm about to hear is really private and important. I need to give my full attention and the assurance of complete confidentiality.*

Authenticity Outside of Marriage

Some women enjoy this kind of intimacy and authenticity with their husbands, and so they don't feel the need to seek it elsewhere, in friendships with other women. Yet there are many aspects of the female experience that are impossible for any man, however sensitive, to fully understand and appreciate. A man may listen actively and respond sympathetically, but he will never truly identify with the emotions, experiences, pressures, and hormones of womanhood. He will never comprehend the lifelong quest to be beautiful, the desperate need to be understood, or the unquenchable desire to nurture. He will never ride the relentless emotional roller coaster of the menstrual cycle or suffer the "private beach parties" (more commonly known as hot flashes) brought on by menopause. We women are complex creatures, and, whether we're married or single, we thrive from sharing life's journey with other women.

Authenticity Is Worth the Awkwardness

Intimacy in our friendships with others comes through sharing—with authenticity—not only our life experiences but also how we think and feel about them. A few years ago, I was scheduled to speak at a women's outreach event in another city. I arrived by plane, Patty met me there, and we stayed in the beautiful home of Andrea, the chairperson of the event. Her efforts to prepare for this outreach were incredible. Andrea and her committee had gone all out. The auditorium was beautifully decorated, and great attention had been given to every detail of the evening.

When I stood up and started to speak, I had the impression that the audience was very reserved. There I was, pouring my heart out, and I might as well have been reciting the alphabet, for the response I was getting. After my presentation, I felt like a failure, and I was sure I had disappointed Andrea.

A few months later, Andrea invited Patty to speak at an event, and she asked me to come along to support her. I wanted to be there for my friend, but I was struggling in my heart. I was dealing with a host of thoughts and emotions I wasn't comfortable feeling, let alone expressing. But I knew I had to tell Patty what was going on inside me, no matter how difficult that would be. I cared far too much about her to leave her guessing as to why I was acting withdrawn.

On the day of the event at which Patty was to speak, the two of us had lunch together, and I finally bared my soul. I explained that, in my heart, I wanted her to do a great job, and I really wanted God to use her powerfully among the women who attended the event. I also confessed that seeing her succeed was going to make another part of me feel bad, because I had done my best just a few months ago, with less than stellar results. It was hard to make eye contact with Patty as I shared my feelings. I certainly wasn't proud of them.

> Authenticity in friendship is not always easy, but it is the only path to mutual trust.

I will never forget Patty's response. It was such a gift. She didn't prop up my wilted self-esteem by trying to convince me that my presentation had been better than I remembered it or even by reminding me that the results of my ministry are the responsibility of the Holy Spirit. I already knew that. She just thanked me for being real. And the seeds of jealousy in our relationship were immediately uprooted. Something that easily could have put a damper on our relationship for years ended up knitting our hearts together more profoundly than ever before, and it was all because of authenticity.

Instead of showing Patty the "me" I wished I was, I showed her the real me. It felt uncomfortable to be so exposed, with my selfish thoughts and tainted emotions laid bare on the table, but it also felt comforting because I knew that the "me" Patty was accepting and loving, even in this messy situation, was the real me.

Authenticity in friendship is not always easy, but it is the only way for us to know and be known. It is the only path to mutual trust. There is very little satisfaction or comfort in a relationship between two people pretending to be people they aren't. That's called role-play, not relationship. And it's false and unfulfilling. What's the point?

Being authentic enables one real, unmasked heart to bond with another, so that both individuals experience the joy of unqualified acceptance.

The Ability to Be at Ease

When we're traveling together, Patty and I tend to stumble around the airport—I think I'm following her; she thinks I know where I'm going; both of us talk nonstop the entire time. We call it the "blonde leading the blonde." We'll sometimes stand in a stationary elevator for five minutes or more, chatting away, until we finally realize that neither of us pushed a button. I suppose it's that we enjoy being together so immensely that the task at hand always seems secondary, whether it's catching a plane or arriving at a speaking engagement on time.

It's a wonderful thing to feel so at ease in another's presence that you get lost in the moment. What a joy to be known so completely—and to be confident in being accepted—that you never give a second thought to how your words or actions may be received.

Extreme "At Ease"

Several years ago, Patty and I drove to Montana to speak at a women's conference. We traveled there armed with several assumptions—faulty ones, as it ended up—about the dress code and the accommodations. First of all, the venue was located five hours south of my home, in Calgary, and we assumed that the weather would be at least as warm as it was where I lived. We also knew that the event was to be rather sizable, with more than three hundred women in attendance, and figured it would be held in a large conference center equipped with all of the modern conveniences.

Wrong, wrong, wrong! I knew that Montana has its own unique and wonderfully outdoorsy culture, but it was not what this city girl was expecting. For starters, were you aware that Montana highways have no posted speed limit? We quickly learned why: you could drive like a maniac all day and all night and never run into anyone, because there is no one else there. I'm so glad we didn't have car trouble or run out of gas. We might have perished right there on the side of the road and been dead for weeks before one living soul discovered us.

Suffice it to say that the conference venue was remote. The flocks of wild turkeys on the sides of the road should have tipped us off that we were heading for a rustic setting. We pulled in to the rutted driveway of the retreat center and found the conference delegates wandering the grounds dressed in sweat suits, jeans, and winter jackets. Of course, we had missed the memo, and were attired in business suits and high heels, with no winter wear whatsoever.

The main meeting room, where I delivered my presentations, was heated by a single wood-burning stove. During each session, as many women as could fit virtually piled on top of one another around the stove. The rest of us just froze.

Every evening, when Patty and I had retreated to the little cottage we were sharing, we would be so cold that we were prepared to do just about anything to warm up. So, we would fill the bathtub with the hottest water available, put our bathing suits on, and climb in…together. We were so glad for the warmth, it didn't seem that weird.

Sometimes, when I'm making my travel arrangements, the scheduler will ask me, "Do you mind sharing a room with Patty?" When this happens, I just think, *If you only knew.*

Ease That Transcends Circumstances and Survives Conflicts

Nineteenth-century writer Dinah Craik's description of friendship is poetic and profound:

Oh! the blessing it is to have a friend to whom one can speak fearlessly on any subject; with whom one's deepest as well as one's most foolish thoughts come out simply and safely. Oh, the comfort—the inexpressible comfort of feeling safe with a person—having neither to weigh thoughts nor measure words, but pouring all right out, just as they are, chaff and grain together, certain that a faithful hand will take and sift them, keep what is worth keeping, and with the breath of kindness blow the rest away.[1]

Feeling at ease with someone is a quality of friendship that enables us to enjoy each other's presence, no matter our mood. We can be talkative or quiet, silly or serious, without apology or explanation. We don't have to put our best foot forward, put on a happy face, or put on our makeup. We can laugh, sleep, pray, cry, go on a tirade—whatever we need to do, we can do, confident that we are known well enough and accepted fully enough to just be. No editing necessary.

Of course, even the best of friends may irritate one another from time to time. That's only natural. But two best friends who are at ease with each other can deal honestly with conflict, whether it's a minor tiff or a major argument. They can speak candidly and say, "Are we okay? Have I done something to bother or offend you?" or, on the other side, "You know that I love you, but when you do _____ (whatever it was that bothered or offended), I feel _____." And they can discuss the situation freely until they reach a mutual understanding.

Reconciliation is not always immediate, of course. Recently Patty and I were away together for a ministry project. We worked hard, pushing ourselves far past the point of feeling like quitting. On our final day together, we redoubled our efforts, knowing that

1. Dinah Mulock Craik, *A Life for a Life* (Leipzig: Bernhard Tauchnitz, 1859), 270.

in a few short hours, I had to get on a plane, she had to get in her car, and whatever we hadn't accomplished would have to wait until the next date we could commit to work together. By the time we had to pack up and vacate the suite we'd been sharing, both of us were "just done." And what had been a wonderful week of harmonious collaboration culminated suddenly in a sharp disagreement over something so trivial, it is simply too embarrassing to explain.

I tried to make light of the situation, but Patty was having none of it. I had unknowingly pushed her buttons, touching a sore spot I hadn't known was there. In the heat of the moment, she told me that I had a way of making her feel inferior, and that, to her, it felt intentional. She was in no mood to hear an explanation from me. So, I did what I needed to do: I simply apologized for stirring feelings of inferiority in her and asked her to let me know the next time it happened. I said that I needed to learn to be aware of the sensitivity in her—and the insensitivity in me. Several minutes later, after our tempers had calmed, Patty apologized to me, as well, and confessed that her reaction had been exacerbated by her exhaustion.

With that, the dark cloud blew over, and we were ready to enjoy a relaxing lunch together before going our separate ways. If we had neglected to address the disagreement immediately and identify its source, there is no way we could have continued to be at ease with each other. I would have been left wondering what on earth I had said or done to ignite the sparks, and Patty would have retreated from me for being so insensitive. Because we talked it out, we know each other better, and we can be better friends to each other. She can feel safe with me, confident that I care about her heart.

Being with certain people is just hard work. We try hard to always say the right thing and to avoid doing the wrong thing.

We fear causing offense or giving the wrong impression. How refreshing it is to be with someone with whom we can relax and be at ease! Like wrapping ourselves in a fuzzy old bathrobe after a day spent wearing a scratchy wool sweater, spending time with a friend with whom we are at ease is a comfort to cherish in a world of prickly people and abrasive relationships.

Affirmation

Most people on this planet are suffering from affirmation deprivation. Commendations just aren't part of our daily vocabulary. If an employee is consistently on time for work, should he expect to hear his boss say something like, "Way to go! I've been meaning to applaud you for being punctual every day"? Not at all. But you'd better believe his boss will say something if the employee is habitually late!

Sadly, much more attention is devoted to personal shortcomings than successes. Scarcely anyone seems to pay attention to a job well done. We rarely recognize or affirm the well-honed skills or commendable character qualities of others. Why is it that we are programmed to notice and name one another's shortcomings while downplaying or flat-out disregarding their strengths? Most people seem to be affirmation-challenged on the giving and receiving ends alike.

The Gift of Affirmation

The act of affirming someone means noticing her and validating who she is and what she does. And it's one of the most precious gifts we can ever give. My friend Wendy is excellent at affirming. She believes I can do more than I think I can do and continually encourages me to attempt great things. You see, God has given

> The act of affirming someone is one of the most precious gifts we can ever give.

me big dreams, and I am passionate about them. It's not that I believe my talents are so big or so plentiful. It's just that I live with this overwhelming desire to make a difference. And so, I dream big. But when I share my dreams with others, many of them look at me as if to say, "Who do you think you are?" Not Wendy. She says, "You can do that! When are you going to get started?"

Each of us needs someone to believe in us to help us reach our potential, to take all that we have as far as we can go. For some, this person is a parent, cheering from the sidelines of their soccer game, even in sub-zero temperatures. For others, it's a coach who draws out their talent, or a teacher who recognizes them as an academic "diamond in the rough." And for others, it's a close friend who is never farther than a phone call away.

A dear friend of mine has gone through many rocky patches in her marriage, times of deep loneliness, when the only words of affirmation she received came from me. It has been a privilege to be the cheerleader in her life; to say things like, "You're a great mom!" and "You look gorgeous today!" and "That was a really difficult situation, and you handled it beautifully. I am so proud of you!"

Proverbs 18:4 says, *"A person's words can be life-giving water."* We blossom like flowers nourished by fresh water and warm sunshine when someone expects the best of us and encourages us along the path in the pursuit of a goal, whether it's a big endeavor or simply the survival of another day.

Break the Chain of Negativity

How many times in any given day are we told, either subtly or overtly, "You don't measure up"? How many times do we say it to ourselves? According to psychologists, it takes seven positive inputs to counteract one negative input, which we store so deeply in the recesses of our memories. The reason is that once we have determined what we believe to be the truth about ourselves, we go around collecting data that supports our belief, while we discount all evidence to the contrary.

How crucial, then, that we love one another by being truth tellers in the most positive and uplifting sense!

A few months ago, I received a most unexpected note of affirmation. My surprise was equal at the source and content alike. It came via e-mail from a casual friend I rarely see, and it expressed sentiments I had no idea she held. It was like a gentle rain on parched and thirsty ground. It read as follows:

Hi Donna,

Some of my deepest thoughts occur as I'm blow-drying my hair in the morning...a strange confession, I know. This morning, I was reminded of a friend's funeral earlier this year. A neighbor/friend of Mick [the deceased, who passed away at seventy-five years of age] spoke of how he had been challenged as a young executive many years ago to find someone whose life exhibited qualities that he would like to foster in his own life. Twenty years ago, he chose Mick without revealing it to anyone...until the funeral. At length he spoke of Mick's many character qualities that he admired and tried to emulate ever the years. Sadly, Mick never knew about this. So, I began thinking of whom, in my circle of friends and acquaintances, I would choose.

Without a doubt, it is you. There are many things that I admire about you: your passion for God, which gives you depth of character; your frankness, which is so refreshing; your ability to articulate; your love for your family; your sense of humor; your desire to look good/ fit without being obsessive-compulsive; the fact that you strive to put boundaries in your life; your desire to keep growing and encouraging others to do the same; your passion for lost souls, having been wounded and allowing God to use that for good in your life...I could go on and on, but I don't want to bore you (ha ha).

However, the most obvious is that you look just like your Father (God), and that is the highest compliment and goal any of us can have, I believe. One of the reasons I am telling you all this is I am realizing that waiting till a funeral to affirm a friend is a tragedy.

She is absolutely right—about that last part, anyway. I know, because I learned the hard way, remember?

Affirming a friend—noticing and naming her strengths and accomplishments—can refuel a weary soul, keeping her moving forward or even unleashing her potential. Affirmation may not come naturally, at first. Like almost every aspect of relationships, affirmation involves some risk. But when we put our positive thoughts into words for the benefit of our friends, it makes a huge difference in their lives and gives them the courage to keep going, to take risks, and to become all that they can be.

THE BLONDE
LEADING THE BLONDE

Questions for Reflection and Discussion

1. On a scale of 1 (not at all) to 10 (completely), how authentic are you with your friends regarding your thoughts and feelings?

2. Would you agree that even happily married women still need close female friends? Why or why not?

3. Recall a time when you took a risk and expressed difficult feelings with a friend who accepted and encouraged you. How did it change your relationship with that person?

4. Do you have a friend with whom you feel especially at ease? How do the two of you handle conflict in your relationship?

5. The Bible compares affirmation to physical necessities, such as food and water. Proverbs 18:20 says, *"Words satisfy the soul as food satisfies the stomach; the right words on a person's lips bring satisfaction."* Think of a time when a word of affirmation gave you the courage to reach for a challenging goal. Who affirmed you, what was said, and how did it affect you?

6. When was the last time you affirmed someone in your circle of friends? Whom can you affirm today?

5

A SOFT PLACE TO FALL

The next two traits of friendship we will discuss are acceptance and accountability. These qualities are related, although not always comfortably so. One is warm and fuzzy, while the other is often perceived as harsh and confrontational. One makes us feel good; the other we would rather avoid at all costs. One represents grace, the other, truth.

Acceptance says, "I love you just the way you are, so I won't try to change you, but I will support you in your efforts to change." Accountability says, "I love you too much to let you continue unchallenged in this way. I will courageously call out the best in you and be a truth teller in your life."

Acceptance and Accountability Work Hand in Hand

There was a time when the border between these two important traits of friendship became a bit blurred for me. My husband and I were close friends with a couple whose spending habits drove me crazy. Because the four of us spent a lot of time together, took vacations together, and were generally apprised of each other's significant decisions and major purchases, we had seen them at every point on the cycle of spending above and beyond their means and then digging their way out of debt. To me, they seemed fiscally irresponsible.

Before I go on with this story, you need to know something about me. I have a problem. Everyone knows that the first step to recovery is acknowledging that you have a problem, so here it is: "My name is Donna, and I am a control-aholic."

The good news is, I'm in the recovery stage. But the fact of my problem first became clear to me many years ago, at a family camp we attended because Randy was the featured speaker. Our daughters, Kendall and Kevann, were still very young, and so I would put them to bed and stay with them in the room while Randy stayed out and spoke to the other attendees. This was hardly an inconvenience to me; I love to read, and I had packed plenty of books. But then, the unthinkable happened. I ran out of books. In sheer desperation, I picked up a book I had bought for Randy. I had not planned on reading this book because I didn't think it applied to me. The book was called *Imperative People: For Those Who Must Be in Control*.

Can you grasp the irony here? You know you are controlling when you purchase self-help books for other people. But I didn't catch on until, to my horror, I saw myself reflected in the pages of that book. As I worked my way through the chapters, I began to realize that I was not responsible to "fix" or change Randy or anyone else. I was and still am responsible for my own thoughts, attitudes, emotions, and behavior—no one else's.

Extend Unconditional Acceptance

The apostle Paul instructs us, *"Accept each other just as Christ has accepted you; then God will be glorified"* (Romans 15:7). Jesus doesn't pressure me to become like Him in order for Him to accept me. No, He extends His grace to me without conditions. Learning to extend this grace to others, and learning to cooperate with Jesus as He changes me, has taken me to a higher level in all of my relationships.

> Learning to extend grace to others has taken me to a higher level in all of my relationships.

This lesson came several years after my decision to offer what I believed to be extremely helpful advice regarding my friend's finances. My friend—we'll call her Jane—had just landed a part-time job, and I asked her, ever so tactfully, if she would like me to hold her accountable to use her new source of income to pay off the debt she and her husband had incurred. She replied with an emphatic "No." Not "Let me think about it" or "I'll talk to my husband about it" or even "I'll pray about it." Just "No."

Can you imagine? Instead of being grateful for my concern, she was actually offended!

Of course, I know now that I was totally out of line—not because it's necessarily inappropriate for one friend to challenge another on as personal an issue as finances, but because my "help" was offered in a spirit of judgment, not acceptance.

Offer Guidance with Grace

Here is another nugget of wisdom from the apostle Paul: *"We will speak the truth in love, growing in every way more and more like Christ, who is the head of his body, the church"*

(Ephesians 4:15 NLT07). It is never appropriate to speak the truth without love, to confront without grace, or to hold someone accountable without compassion and acceptance.

Grace is unconditional love and acceptance. Dr. Henry Cloud defines it as "unbroken, uninterrupted, unearned, accepting relationship." Grace is a critical component of every thriving friendship. But alone, it isn't enough. All of us long to experience love with muscles strong enough to bear the weight of the truth about us without giving up on us.

There is no greater demonstration of the marriage of grace and truth than God's love and acceptance of His fallen creation. As Romans 5:8 reminds us, *"But God showed his great love for us by sending Christ to die for us while we were still sinners."* God didn't wait for us to clean up our act before He accepted us.

> *How blessed is God! And what a blessing he is! He's the Father of our Master, Jesus Christ, and takes us to the high places of blessing in him. Long before he laid down earth's foundations, he had us in mind, had settled on us as the focus of his love, to be made whole and holy by his love. Long, long ago he decided to adopt us into his family through Jesus Christ. (What pleasure he took in planning this!) He wanted us to enter into the celebration of his lavish gift-giving by the hand of his beloved Son.* (Ephesians 1:3–6 MSG)

Our heavenly Father didn't demand that we reform ourselves in order to be worthy of His love. He knew that we could never solve our own sin problem, so He accepted us, just as we were, even in our sin. It wasn't that He didn't mind our sin; it disgusted Him. Consider this graphic portrayal by the prophet Isaiah: *"We are all infected and impure with sin. When we proudly display our righteous deeds, we find they are but filthy rags"* (Isaiah 64:6).

Isaiah wasn't referring to dishrags or even dust rags. The term he employed was used to designate soiled menstrual rags.

No, it wasn't that Christ was not disgusted by our sins. It was that His love—His limitless grace and mercy—was far more powerful.

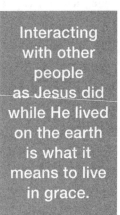

Interacting with other people as Jesus did while He lived on the earth is what it means to live in grace.

Knowing that God has dealt with our sin by offering us forgiveness through the shedding of Jesus' blood, shouldn't we be able to accept ourselves? And if the holy God of heaven could accept us *"while we were still sinners,"* shouldn't one sinner be able to do the same for a fellow sinner? Interacting with other people as Jesus did while He lived on the earth is what it means to live in grace.

Through the pages of the Bible, we can follow the path Jesus forged from one broken, damaged human being to another. He was criticized for associating with "sinners," but, rather than denying it, He affirmed that it was part of His purpose.

> *While Jesus was having dinner at Matthew's house, many tax collectors and "sinners" came and ate with him and his disciples. When the Pharisees saw this, they asked his disciples, "Why does your teacher eat with tax collectors and 'sinners'?" On hearing this, Jesus said, "It is not the healthy who need a doctor, but the sick. But go and learn what this means: 'I desire mercy, not sacrifice.' For I have not come to call the righteous, but sinners."* (Matthew 9:10–13 NIV)

Jesus wasn't naïve. He knew about Zacchaeus' greed and Mary Magdalene's scarlet-lettered past. He predicted Peter's betrayal and even Judas's treacherous plans. And still He offered the gift of relationship. He accepted those who sought His grace. It is only when truth is spoken in an atmosphere of grace that true intimacy is possible.

Convict with Compassion

My daughters are both gymnasts. Their strength and flexibility astonish me. Even more amazing are the risks they take in the course of a routine. (By the way, I find "routine" to be a ridiculous name for a series of life- and limb-jeopardizing contortions. The moves they do are most certainly not part of my daily routine!) Thankfully, the thick, cushioned mats positioned beneath the parallel bars and the balance beam mitigate the consequences when those risks become realities and the girls fall.

Those mats are an apt illustration of what we are to be for the friends we hold accountable. If we feel compelled, by our love and concern, to speak truth into the life of a friend, we must also offer a "mat" of grace for her to fall on.

Patty and I are quite candid in our comments to each other. We have shared so much that we know where one another's weak spots are located, and we love each other enough to say what needs to be said.

On another trip we took together, Patty made several offhand comments about how I'd forgotten various details and failed to catch parts of our conversations. We tease each other a lot, so I didn't realize that she was subtly pointing out a flaw of mine until she made a retort later, partly in jest, about my needing to take a "skilled listener course."

Finally, I got the hint. I said, "Do you think I'm a poor listener?"

She replied with a question of her own, which was more than adequate: "Do you really want to know?" *Ouch.*

In the balance of that conversation, I learned, through the eyes of someone who loves me exactly as I am but loves me too much to let me stay there, something about myself and the way others perceive me.

I frequently reflect on this bare exchange between Patty and me. I think about her question—how she invited me to ask her to tell the truth, thereby graciously preparing me for something I'd probably rather not hear. I remember the way I inwardly steeled myself against the pain I knew would come from hearing the truth, even as I said, "Yes, I really do want to know." And I remember the way my friend spoke the truth in love, following the instructions found in Ephesians 4:15.

Both of us chose the hard thing that day—Patty, the messiness of tender meddling, and I, the abrasiveness of truth. I have many friends who are fun to be with and will tell me the truth I want to hear, but rare indeed is the friend who will risk wounding me with the truth I *need* to hear.

Let Compassion Rule

Knowing the truth about ourselves frees us to grow into the people God wants us to be. Jesus made a profound statement when He said, *"You will know the truth, and the truth will set you free"* (John 8:32). Every self-defeating behavior is accompanied by a lie. If we are bound by these deceptions, we will continue in our destructive patterns. Grasping the truth about ourselves, God, and others makes us gloriously free. If we will let Him, He will use our friends as agents of that kind of change in us.

Proverbs 27:17 says, *"As iron sharpens iron, a friend sharpens a friend."* I'm no blacksmith, but I have a feeling that being either piece of iron in this scenario is painful. The friction involved creates heat and polishes our rough edges. But the tools that emerge from the trauma are smooth and sharp and far more useful to their master than they were before.

As previously mentioned, I have walked with a dear friend through deep waters in her marriage. When she looks back on those years, she is grateful for the encouragement I offered her. But what she talks about more often, all these years later, is how glad she is that I was not always on her side.

When you're in the midst of overwhelming pain, it's pretty tough to keep true north in the windshield. In those times when her perspective was lost in a storm of emotions, I would say, for example, "I think you're wrong about his motives," or "He can't give you what he doesn't have," or something else to help her see beyond her own wall of grief.

It would have been easier for me to agree with her and say, "What a jerk!" Frankly, I wanted to kill him, too. But what she needed most—even more than affirmation or comfort—was truth. When she and her husband awakened to the truth in their hearts, it was ultimately what saved their marriage and transformed it from an imminent train wreck into a loving, growing, sometimes struggling, testimony of God's passionate desire to restore relationships.

> Being friends doesn't mean always agreeing with each other.

Being friends doesn't mean always agreeing with each other. It definitely doesn't mean supporting decisions or behaviors that are not in the other person's best interest. Sometimes, it means offering another perspective. Sometimes, it means confrontation. Occasionally, it involves holding the other person to a higher standard than she has set for herself. But any kind of intervention must always be for her sake and always offered in a spirit of loving acceptance and grace.

When my friend Kate was asked to participate in her best friend's wedding, she was conflicted out of concern for the bride-to-be. She didn't think it was a good match. While Kate's best friend was bringing a good education, a great career, and a nice nest egg to the marriage, her chosen partner was bringing a needy child, a history of failed careers, and a load of debt. Kate suspected that her forty-something, childless friend might be more in love with the little boy than his father. She also feared that love, and a desire to be loved, had blinded her to the many faults of her fiancé.

The last thing Kate wanted to do was rain reality down on her friend's joyful parade, but she knew that because she loved her, she needed to tell her the truth. So, she took a risk and expressed her concern to the bride-to-be about the path she was choosing. Having done that—and having failed to dissuade her—Kate put on her dress and stood by her best friend as she tied the knot. She was still standing by her best friend less than one year later when her marriage, her beloved stepson, and her life savings were gone, and she needed a place to start over. She moved into Kate's basement and lived there for a year, until she got her feet under her again. Kate's actions are the model of acceptance with accountability.

If you love your friends, tell them the truth. Say what needs to be said. But do it with tender words and with arms wide open, your heart filled not with judgment but care. Always keep in mind this truth from 1 Corinthians 13:

> *If you love someone, you will be loyal to him no matter what the cost. You will always believe in him, always expect the best of him, and always stand your ground in defending him.* (1 Corinthians 13:7 TLB)

A friendship with accountability is two people lovingly and courageously calling out the best in each other and being truth tellers in each other's lives.

Assistance

Just like accountability, the trait of assistance in friendship requires great sensitivity. To offer assistance without coming across as condescending, we need to be attuned to the emotions and needs of our friends so that we may both recognize when they need help and discern how to go about providing it.

The relationship between intimacy and effective assistance comes across in Ecclesiastes 4:9–10:

> *Two people can accomplish more than twice as much as one; they get a better return for their labor. If one person falls, the other can reach out and help. But people who are alone when they fall are in real trouble.*

In our travels together, the accommodations Patty and I have experienced have run the gamut. On some trips, we stay in luxury hotels where we're treated like queens. On other occasions, we're put up at camps where the facilities are, shall we say, rustic. I remember one such place, in particular—in its previous life, it could have been a prison work camp. As we opened the tinfoil door of the prehistoric ATCO trailer that was to be our home for the weekend, we had the distinct sense that we would not be alone. Our disconcerting impression was that our roommates might be furry and four-legged. I was quietly praying that we wouldn't have any face-to-face encounters with them. But not Patty. Oh, no! When it comes to vermin, her motto should be, "Go big or go home." With the ardor of a televangelist, she was ceremoniously casting them out in the name of Jesus.

Whether in a Hilton or a hick town, it means so much to me to have the company and assistance of my ministry partner and friend. Patty is the kind of person who sees what needs to be done and just does it. She prays with me before my speaking engagements, and she prays for me while I speak. Early on in my career, she kept me from fleeing the scene while I nervously waited to be introduced. She has bailed me out in the sound booth, seconds before I'm to go on stage, when it has become clear that the technician isn't going to catch the vision, regardless of how many times I repeat the sequence of elements in my presentation. On those occasions, I have been able to look up from the stage and relax because I know that with Patty back there, no cues will be missed, and everything will run smoothly.

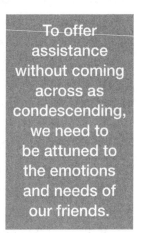

To offer assistance without coming across as condescending, we need to be attuned to the emotions and needs of our friends.

Then, there have been times when I've finished speaking and some poor, burdened soul comes to me, looking for wisdom, but God doesn't give me the words; He gives them to Patty. I think we make a great team in ministry. I am much more effective with Patty than without her.

Usually, at the end of a demanding weekend of ministry, I am completely worn out, wrung dry of all energy. After saying the final good-bye and giving the last hug, I drag my sorry self back to the hotel room, dreading the process of packing up and loading the car, only to find that the work is already done—by none other than my friend Patty. So often, the assistance she offers takes place in the shadows, which makes it all the sweeter when it comes into the light.

Scriptural Assistance

The Bible has a lot to say about the importance of assisting one another. Galatians 6:2 commands us, *"Carry each other's burdens, and in this way you will fulfill the law of Christ"* (NIV). The law of Christ is to love God with our whole being and to love others as we love ourselves. (See Matthew 22:36–40.) To offer assistance to others, we ought to do for them what we would desire someone else do for us, were we in the same situation.

At times, our burdens seem like ten-pound sacks of flour that we manage to carry, albeit barely. At other times, they feel like crushing loads that we are utterly incapable of shouldering alone.

Kelly and Hanna were best friends. They shared many secrets, including the loneliness Hanna was experiencing in her marriage. What Hanna never would have guessed in a million years is that they were also sharing her husband.

Kelly would be consoling Hanna and offering advice to help her marriage one day, and actively participating in its destruction the next.

When Hanna found out about the affair, she was devastated. The simultaneous betrayal by her husband and her best friend was almost more than she could handle, emotionally and physically. After weeping for days, she collapsed from dehydration. When she awoke again, she was lying in bed, hooked up to an IV, in the home of a couple who had been good friends in the past and were to become her lifeline in the future.

As Hanna looks back on that painful time, there is a lot she can't remember. Yet through the fog of her depression emerge images of this caring couple bringing her groceries, hugging her distraught kids, making meals for her family, and coaxing her to get out of bed when all she wanted to do was give up and sleep away the pain. They did this not just for a week or two but for six months.

Today, Hanna's heart is healed, and her marriage is vital. What an amazing testimony to God's grace expressed through the body of Christ! In remembering the sacrifice of these precious friends, Hanna says, "We never would have made it without them. They were the hands and feet of God to me."

The Sacrifice of Service

At times, bearing another's burden means putting her needs above our own. It means making the choice to keep working, even though we've earned the right to relax. To walk into an emotionally charged situation when we would rather sit back and watch a sitcom. To love and care for another as we love and care for ourselves. That's the law of Christ, and by sharing a friend's burden, we are fulfilling that law.

Again, being a true friend involves both risk and sacrifice. Sometimes, it may be more challenging to offer acceptance than to withdraw. It is always daunting to hold someone accountable; we'd much rather ignore a fault, even if it's going to wreak damage in her life. And it certainly comes more naturally to take care of our own interests rather than setting our interests aside in order to assist someone else. But this is the journey God has called us to. It's a journey of self-sacrifice and self-discovery, of grace and growth, of freedom and fulfillment. How does one begin this journey? Let's explore the trailhead together.

A SOFT PLACE TO FALL

Questions for Reflection and Discussion

1. When is it appropriate to hold someone accountable?

2. How does God's acceptance of us when we were sinners demonstrate the tension between grace and truth? (See Isaiah 64:6; Romans 5:8.)

3. How does God use friends to free each other? (See John 8:32; Proverbs 27:17; James 5:16.) Can you think of an example from your own experience?

4. Ecclesiastes 4:9–10 says, "*Two people can accomplish more than twice as much as one; they get a better return for their labor. If one person falls, the other can reach out and help. But people who are alone when they fall are in real trouble.*" Recall a time when you fell into trouble. Who was there to help you up? What did that person do that was particularly meaningful?

5. Which of the three traits of friendship we discussed in this chapter—acceptance, accountability, and assistance—do you most need today? Which is the hardest for you to offer to others? Why?

Part III

THE PATH OF FRIENDSHIP

6

HOW TO BUILD A FRIENDSHIP

In the fall of 2003, Randy and I traveled to Haiti for the first time. It was going to be the trip of a lifetime. Ever since making the decision to go, I had experienced a mixture of eager anticipation and dread. I looked forward to the trip because I love to travel. Experiencing new things and making new memories really excites me. At the same time, I dreaded the trip because I knew I would be stretched and possibly broken by inevitable exposure to some of the worst poverty and profoundest misery in the world. I also felt a degree of apprehension at the prospect of spending the entire span of nine days with nine other people, seven of whom I either barely knew or had never met at all.

I was pretty sure I could handle my husband and my good friend Karen 24/7, but I had no idea about the others. The only thing we all had in common was a desire to learn more about the work of an organization called Compassion International, which seeks to alleviate the suffering of impoverished children worldwide.

Our group met at the airport very early in the morning. It was amazing how quickly everyone's true colors emerged. There was Allan, the highly motivated, independent businessman, always two steps ahead of the group's leader, who kept admonishing us, "Come on, people!" There was Dave, the laid-back radio DJ, who was last to arrive at the airport and showed a consistent lack of punctuality for the duration of the trip. Then, there was John, better known among us as "Inspector Gadget." Even the most diligent Boy Scout could never have been so well prepared for every possible scenario. John endured a lot of good-natured abuse from the rest of the group, but we would have been in trouble many times if it hadn't been for his amazing, seemingly bottomless backpack.

Even before boarding the plane, Randy and I had quietly assessed the temperament types of the people who would be our traveling companions for the next nine days. We found ourselves wondering, "What will it be like to live with these people? Will Allan's motivational speeches drive us crazy? Will Dave's dawdling make us late every day? Will John actually generate electricity out of his backpack?"

> Only God could have taken such a diverse group of people and made friends out of us.

Only God could have taken such a diverse group of people and made friends out of us. We varied vastly in age, background, and temperament, but all of us were Christ followers bent on learning, through this eye-opening adventure, our responsibility to the poor.

There is something powerful about common experiences, about seeing the same vistas and sharing the same vantage point. Whatever reservations I'd had about Allan disappeared when I heard him weep and pray over the overwhelming need of the Haitian people. Any frustrations with DJ Dave's "Hakuna Matata" concept of time evaporated as I watched the little children flock to him to be cuddled, teased, and tickled. And John certainly redeemed himself by giving me a camping towel and one of those metallic emergency blankets after a near-drowning experience that we now refer to as our "Caribbean cruise."

After we had laughed together, cried together, prayed together, and feared for our lives together, our hearts were interwoven in a most amazing way. Now we had something in common beyond our commitment to Jesus. Or, to put that more precisely, we had something in common *through* our commitment to Jesus. We had made memories together, and we were totally passionate about Compassion International and their work of "releasing children from poverty in Jesus' name."

This common passion has brought us together occasionally since our trip to Haiti and has also sustained our friendships, however unlikely they were. The beautiful thing about relationships built on shared experience is that, over time, they become less and less about the task or purpose from which they originated and more and more about the enjoyment of one another's company—the pleasure of being together.

Over time, we've collected common experiences from "doing" life together, and our friendships have gradually deepened. Our shared history has provided a context for trust to be built; we have learned, from the patterns of the past, that these people are going to be there for us and help us, whether we're moving into a new house, moving past the pain of a job loss, or moving through the tumultuous waters of our marriage. We will stand by each other when the baby moves out, the in-laws move in, and time moves on.

These are the people who will genuinely share our joy on the mountaintops of life, and they will be the ones to pick up the pieces when our lives fall apart. We are committed to each other for the long haul. And the power of this kind of relationship is multiplied when it is shared by a group of friends.

A Circle of Friends

We often hear about the negative effects of peer pressure or "groupthink," but the influence of a group of true friends can prove very positive. A small group of close, committed friends can help one another become who they really want to be, even when they lack the strength or conviction to pursue those identities on their own. When everyone is pulling in the same direction, like a rowing team, they take each other farther and faster, over calm waters and stormy seas alike. If one rower weakens and her arms grow slack, the boat may lose some momentum, but it keeps moving forward and making progress.

Strengthened from All Sides

On one occasion, when I was teaching the biblically based life management course I wrote, called "10 Smart Things Women Can Do to Build a Better Life," a young woman named Michelle attended. She was into self-improvement and thought it sounded like an interesting self-help course.

Through the sessions, Michelle came to faith in Jesus, and her decision to live for Him became a powerful catalyst for change in her family. Soon, her husband, Oden, also entered into a relationship with Jesus, and the two of them publicly dedicated their three young children to God.

Not only did Michelle understand that her friendship with God was important, but she also seized the opportunity to join a small group of young mothers who met regularly to pray together and encourage one another in their faith as they toiled through a busy phase of life.

One Sunday after church, Michelle and her family stopped at the home of some friends. The adults visited briefly, raising their voices to compete with the background noise of excited little children playing and chasing each other through the house.

Someone asked, "Where's Raelyn?"

Last seen, Michelle and Oden's little nineteen-month-old daughter had been doing her best to keep up with the bigger kids.

It turned out that nobody knew where she was, and so, with mild concern, they began to search the house and yard. Michelle's alarm mounted by the minute. Soon she and Oden grew frantic, and the police were called. When their little girl was found, she was floating facedown in a nearby swimming pool, beneath the plastic cover. She was rushed to the hospital, but all efforts to breathe life back into her tiny body proved futile.

In this time of unfathomable sorrow, who did Michelle call on? Not her parents, not her pastor, not a grief counselor—she called her small group. Lindy, the group leader, and other women from the group met Michelle at the hospital and surrounded her and her grief-stricken family with loving support. Then, they simply did what needed to be done: making phone calls, doing yard work, baking, babysitting, hugging, crying, loving, listening. Michelle's friends wanted to ease the burden of shock, guilt, and agony that Michelle and Oden bore. Of course, only God can bring true comfort, and these women knew that. But, just as they had observed in the biblical example of Jonathan helping his friend David, these women helped their friend Michelle reach for God.

The story I'm referring to—the story of the beautiful friendship between Jonathan and David—is recorded in the book of 1 Samuel. David had just slain the overgrown bully Goliath, thereby resuscitating the reputation of Israel's God and her king, Saul. After being congratulated by the grateful king, David was introduced to Saul's son Jonathan. First Samuel tells it like this:

> *After David had finished talking with Saul, he met Jonathan, the king's son. There was an immediate bond of love between them, and they became the best of friends. From that day on Saul kept David with him at the palace and wouldn't let him return home. And Jonathan made a special vow to be David's friend, and he sealed the pact by giving him his robe, tunic, sword, bow, and belt.* (1 Samuel 18:1–4)

There is more to this passage than you might catch at first glance. If anyone had reason to be jealous of David, it was Jonathan, the heir apparent to the throne. Yet Jonathan felt such an affinity for David, and respected him so much, that he insisted on exchanging his friend's peasant clothing and shepherd's weapons for his own attire—the garments and arms of a prince and soldier. In so doing, Jonathan gave David equal standing with himself before the nation and his father, a move that risked his future position and protection, considering that David had just become Israel's newest "rock star," so to speak.

Jonathan's father was not so generous. In fact, King Saul was an unstable egomaniac who seemed to alternate between loving David and hating him. Eventually, the king became obsessed with the quest to kill his perceived rival. Jonathan was placed in the unenviable position of spy and informant, in order to save his friend from his father's homicidal rampage.

Chapter 23 of 1 Samuel continues with an account of Saul's relentless pursuit. David had been hunted and been running for his life for far too long. He was exhausted, afraid, and sinking quickly into despair. And his friend stepped in. *"And Saul's son Jonathan went to David at Horesh and helped him find strength in God"* (1 Samuel 23:16 NIV).

Just as Jonathan had done in encouraging David, the women from the small group pointed Michelle to God rather than encouraging her to depend on them and their assistance, helpful though it was. They knew that, beyond performing everyday chores and simply gifting her with their presence, the best thing they could do for Michelle was to help her find strength in God. They kept rowing the boat toward the safety of the shoreline when Michelle couldn't even lift an oar.

An excellent illustration of the power of friends is portrayed in the NBC-TV film *A Mother's Courage*, which tells the story of basketball star Isiah Thomas and his mother, Mary Thomas. In one scene, Mary talks to her children about resisting the influence of gangs. She opens up a box of matches, pulls out a single wooden match, and asks one of the children to break it. He does so easily. Then, she takes out ten or twelve matches and asks him to break them all at once. He finds he cannot. And Mary has made her point: one may be weak, but many together are strong.

Alone, Michelle may have been broken, her fresh faith shattered. But, surrounded by a circle of caring friends, she experienced not

> One may be weak, but many together are strong.

only their strength but also the strength of the One who calls them His body.

Going Deeper

Randy and I are part of a small group that began more than seventeen years ago with only three couples. We have a long history of helping one another. For instance, we've moved not one but *two* pianos, and two hide-a-beds, in and out of our basement. You need to have a history with someone before you inflict that kind of punishment on them!

Another part of our shared history is a host of inside jokes. For instance, a couple with the last name Balzun became "the Balzoons" after the wife, Carla, was introduced on the evening news and her name was mispronounced. And when Dale Dyck made the mistake of telling us about a misprint on his business cards, he became, for all eternity, Dak Dyck. And then, there was the time someone mistakenly used the word *amalgamation* instead of *augmentation* to describe a surgical procedure performed on a woman's breasts—a terrible image, I know, but in our group, that one will never, ever die.

Whenever a new member joins our group, it takes quite a bit of time and explaining to get him or her up to speed on our particular brand of humor. It also takes time to develop intimacy and thereby pave a path to trust.

One tool that facilitates the process of connecting was introduced to us by our leader, the now famous Dak Dyck. He calls it the "Question of the Day." We always begin our time together by going around the circle and sharing a brief response to the question, which may be something along these lines: "What is your favorite memory of Christmas?" "Which teacher impacted your life the most and why?" "If you could change one thing about your past, what would it be?"

No one is ever pressured to disclose anything that would cause discomfort or embarrassment. Yet the more open we are—the deeper our forays into each other's experiences—the more we strengthen our foundation of trust and deepen the intimacy of our friendship. Of course, the rules of confidentiality need to be understood, accepted, and observed by everyone in order for this trust to blossom.

A friend of mine has worked extensively with the First Nations people (Aboriginals in Canada) as a public health nurse. After she had spent a significant amount of time among this people group, an elder woman told her about the custom of the red cloth.

In Native culture, red is the color of women because it represents the blood of the menstrual period and of childbirth. A red cloth symbolizes the sharing of women. When the cloth is spread, it is understood that whatever a woman chooses to share from her heart is laid on the cloth for the others present in the circle. Those women may take the wisdom offered for themselves or leave it on the cloth, but they may not take it to share with someone who is not present in the circle. Implicit in the red cloth is the sacred promise of strict confidentiality. When the sharing time is over, the red cloth is folded up, with all of its secrets secure, until the next time the women come together to share.

What a beautiful tradition. And what a lovely, tangible reminder of our sacred responsibility to guard each other's

> Intimacy cannot flourish without trust, and trust takes time to grow.

personal expressions as though they were our own. Intimacy cannot flourish without trust, and trust takes time to grow. It is only as we invest our time, our energy, and our hearts in others, intertwining our stories with theirs over the years, that we build friendships tall and strong enough to shelter us from the harshness of life's storms.

The Seasons of Friendship

Meeting a new friend is like finding a buried treasure. There you were, just slogging through the sand, minding your own business, and then, there she was, twinkling up at you, the sun glinting off of her smooth surfaces. You didn't expect to find a friend in this place, in quite this way, but you smile with serendipitous delight. Everything about her captures your interest, and you drop everything to explore this newfound treasure. You are richer now for having found her, and you just sense that life is going to be so much fuller than it was before.

The delight at finding a new friend feels a lot like the joy that comes when the first flowers begin to push up through the ground after the final frost of winter. For this reason, springtime is an appropriate metaphor for the period of discovery that follows the formation of a friendship. The "spring" of friendship is a time of excitement and freshness. Like a gentle breeze in springtime, a new friend breathes energy into your life, and you feel invigorated by her presence. Her stories are so interesting, her conversation so stimulating, and her humor so engaging. Every encounter is always a delightful surprise.

Then, you move into the summer of your relationship; trust is built, and you begin to experience intimacy. The simple enjoyment of her company morphs into a genuine love of her character.

You've heard most of her stories, and you begin to anticipate her sense of humor. You feel safe with her, and you appreciate her honesty because it helps you to know yourself better and also to grow. You look forward to being together.

As you move into autumn, you've heard her stories so many times, you could tell them yourself...and do a better job. Her flaws, which were invisible in springtime and easily overlooked in summer, have become downright annoying. You start to ask, "Why does she do that?" Maybe she breaks a confidence, hurts your feelings, becomes uncommunicative, or lets you down. You might even begin to wonder why you were so attracted to her in the first place.

In many ways, this season of friendship is like the "seven-year itch" experienced by many married couples. Sadly, it's at this point that many friends make the same mistakes as married couples who pull the plug and file for divorce, judging that the work required to repair the relationship would come at too great a price.

The price to pay is risk—the risk of emotional vulnerability. All relational repair is dangerous. It's one thing to risk baring your heart and sharing your unguarded self with a friend who makes you feel close, safe, and accepted. It's quite another to hazard your heart to someone you're not even sure you still want in your life.

But a woman who doesn't let her guard down, doesn't speak her heart, and doesn't listen to the heart of her friend will never experience the coziness of winter, warmed by the crackling fire of mature relationship. She won't even know if such a state is possible. Many women describe themselves as lonely because they've never gotten to this place. They gave up in autumn and watched their friendships wither and die. All of the friendships God has brought into their lives have come and gone without ever reaching the tranquility of winter because these women have been too afraid to go deeper, where there's a risk of getting hurt and having to work to repair rifts in the relationship.

What a reward is a friendship that has weathered life's storms! Nothing reassures like having a friend who has watched you cloud up and hail but has chosen to stay by your side. There is such comfort in knowing one another's ragged edges and smooth surfaces alike; in knowing, accepting, and loving—and in being known, accepted, and loved—warts and blemishes and all. It's the warts and blemishes that take you deeper still. Even if you discover that your friend "dents" and "rusts" and isn't quite as "shiny" as she once seemed, you'll find that she is a real treasure, after all. Your life is richer with her in it—far richer than you could have imagined in the spring.

HOW TO BUILD A FRIENDSHIP

Questions for Reflection and Discussion

1. When have you had the experience of becoming friends with a group of people over a common experience?

2. Donna used the metaphor of a rowing team to illustrate how friends help one another. Can you remember a time when your "team" kept you moving forward when you lacked the strength yourself?

3. How can you help a friend to find her strength in God, as Jonathan did for David? (See 1 Samuel 23:16.)

4. How important is the principle of the red cloth in a group of friends? Can you recall a time when this principle has been violated by someone you trusted? Have you violated it yourself?

5. How many of your friendships have made it through the seasons, all the way to the maturity of winter? Which season are most of your friendships in now? Can you identify anything specific that has prevented your friendships from reaching maturity?

7

TOXIC FRIENDSHIPS

Someone has wisely said, "Show me your friends, and I'll show you your future." We cannot overestimate the degree to which we are influenced by our traveling companions along the road of life. The Bible says, *"Whoever walks with the wise will become wise; whoever walks with fools will suffer harm"* (Proverbs 13:20). When the writer of Proverbs uses the word "fool," he is referring to someone who has chosen to live without regard for God and His wisdom. A fool is unteachable and arrogant, and if she is a friend, her influence on us can only cause us pain.

Relational Toxins

The difference between a friendship infected with a temporary virus and one poisoned with a deadly toxin has to do with teachability. Someone who recognizes a wrong turn and is willing to make a course correction can still be a great friend. After all, none of us is completely whole this side of heaven. It takes discernment to identify harmful tendencies in a relationship, courage to address them, and strength to walk away when necessary.

Relational toxins, such as envy, gossip, discontentment, and narcissism, are so destructive to friendship that they cannot be tolerated without exacting an enormous toll on both the relationship and the individuals whose hearts are invested.

Envy

Envy is simply wanting what belongs to someone else. Often confused with jealousy, this relational poison is far more insidious. In the words of Joseph Epstein in his book *Envy*:

> The real distinction is that *one is jealous of what one has, envious of what other people have.* Jealousy is not always pejorative; one can after all be jealous of one's dignity, civil rights, honor. Envy, except when used in the emulative sense mentioned by Aristotle, is always pejorative. If jealousy is, in cliché parlance, spoken of as the "green-eyed monster," envy is cross-, squinty-, and blearily red-eyed. Never, to put it very gently, a handsome or good thing, envy.[2]

What an apt description for this ugly, all-consuming longing that leads to very ugly behavior and imparts its ugliness to the individual under its sway. It's this ugly little monster that makes us compare aspects of our own life to the corresponding aspects of someone else's—and to desire them even to the point of wishing ill on the other person. It's the reason we keep score of the accomplishments,

---

2. Joseph Epstein, *Envy: The Seven Deadly Sins* (New York: Oxford University Press, 2003), 4.

opportunities, and assets of others and wish they were are own. Envy is terribly destructive to the individual it possesses and to every relationship where it is allowed a foothold.

> Envy is terribly destructive to the individual it possesses and to every relationship where it is allowed a foothold.

When I met Linda, I loved her immediately. She was fun, positive, generous, and loving. We had so many interests in common that it was easy to spend time together. We also had similar backgrounds, talents, and abilities. When we started meeting together regularly to study the Bible and pray, we kept stumbling all over each other because we were both accustomed to being the leader.

In some ways, being with Linda was like being with myself—the parts of me I really liked. However, as we transitioned from spring to summer and then entered into the "autumn" of our relationship, I began to see in Linda some of the parts of me I didn't like. These were parts that I had, in fact, rejected and always tried my best to keep hidden. Suddenly, being with Linda was like looking in the mirror on a bad hair day. It just wasn't all that pleasant anymore.

Oh, we still laughed together, took walks, and met for coffee, but our conversations, anytime they ventured beneath the surface, became about comparing our strengths and concealing our weaknesses. I noticed that Linda never shared a personal struggle with me unless it had already been resolved. And, though I knew I wasn't being real, either, I had a hard time sharing my weaknesses with someone who was always "excellent," "fantastic," or "fabulous."

Sharing our accomplishments and voicing our opportunities always felt like a competition to me, a kind of grown-up, subtle, sophisticated version of "My dad is stronger than your dad"; "Oh yeah? Well, my dad is richer than your dad." Even as we spoke encouragement to each other, on the inside, I sensed that we both were experiencing envy related to the successes and opportunities of the other.

Whenever we said good-bye, I always left feeling worse about myself than I had before our get-together. I was also frustrated that this friendship, which had once been a source of great joy to me, now left me feeling depleted and sad. I think Linda was feeling the same way, because it suddenly seemed harder to find time to get together.

We did continue to connect, albeit sporadically; after all, we had a long history, as well as the memory of how precious our friendship had once been. Sometimes, weeks would pass without a word from Linda, and I would find myself wondering if it was time to just let this relationship go. But as I prayed about it, God made it clear to me that Linda was in my life for a reason, and He was not willing to release me from this friendship.

I now know that God, in His sovereignty and wisdom, brings people into our lives who shine a spotlight—not intentionally, but just by virtue of who they are—on the places in our hearts that are wounded, calloused, or bruised. The parts of us that we have worked hard to keep hidden are suddenly brought to our attention, and we have to decide how we will respond to the resulting discomfort. Will we drop the relationship and dwell in denial, to avoid the pain of dealing with our shortcomings? Or will we embrace the relationship, grateful for its gift of a heart exposed, and walk a parallel path of reconciliation and personal growth?

Doing the latter means seizing the opportunity afforded by the spotlight of our friend's presence in our lives and introducing the broken places of our souls to Jesus for healing and forgiveness. When we can truly accept, love, and forgive ourselves, then we can do the same for others, even when their flaws are painfully familiar.

I knew I needed to tell Linda how I felt and also ask her if she felt the same way, too. On the day we were to meet, she had no idea what my agenda was, and I waffled all day on whether to take this dreaded risk. I knew it could go very badly. She might take offense at my feelings or, worse, deny the existence of any problem on her part. This is what I feared the most—making myself vulnerable, only to hear her insist that she was "excellent."

I hadn't had a good day, and when it was time to drive to the restaurant to meet Linda, I was irritable and grouchy. I argued with God the whole way about whether this was the time to bring up such a sensitive subject. God won the argument, and I am so grateful that He did.

As I revealed my heart to Linda, she wept and confessed her envy of me, a mutual admission of vulnerability unprecedented in all our years of friendship. We agreed that our relationship was worth keeping, and to make that feasible, we set up some ground rules about the way we were to relate to each other. We had to intentionally direct our conversations toward what was on our hearts, not our calendars. We decided to be real with each other about our feelings and to brave the discomfort of baring our hearts. It didn't happen overnight, but a mutual trust began to evolve, and the act of opening our hearts to each other seemed to give God the space to do the work He had longed to do in both of us.

> The act of opening our hearts to each other seemed to give God the space to do the work He had longed to do in both of us.

For me, that work was a lesson in looking to God for approval instead of trying to please and impress everyone else. It also meant giving up my perfectionism and striving for excellence instead. Having my insecurities waved so blatantly in my face motivated me to ask God to free me from their tyranny.

The healing has been a gradual process that's still taking place. I have been freed from perfectionism and the added stress it causes. I continue to wrestle with "people-pleasing" tendencies from time to time. I am still often tempted to compare myself with others, and when I succumb to the temptation, envy rushes in. But the lesson God taught me through my friendship with Linda reminds me that He wants me to be authentic. I know that He will provide everything He wants me to have, to experience, and to accomplish in order to be the most excellent "me" I can be.

Proverbs 27:4 says, *"Anger is cruel, and wrath is like a flood, but who can survive the destructiveness of jealousy ["envy" KJV]?"* Envy, and the competitive spirit it fosters, is a deadly toxin when mixed with friendship. But it isn't the only one. The Bible speaks of several relational toxins that make the natural growth of healthy friendships impossible. Another of these toxins is gossip.

Gossip

My definition of *gossip* is the sharing of information about other people, true or not, that causes others to think less highly of them.

Let's face it: gossip can be fun. When we cast someone else in a negative light, we are unconsciously comparing ourselves with that person—and subtly asserting our superiority, which strokes the ego. But the act of comparing is a toxic practice when it comes to friendships. Someone always comes out looking inferior or feeling belittled.

I have participated in my share of gossip, but I have learned to wean myself off of friendships with people for whom gossip is a popular pastime. I do this for two specific reasons. The first is purely selfish: why should I trust a person with the cluttered closets of my life when she goes about airing the dirty laundry of everyone she knows? The Bible backs up my reasoning: *"A gossip tells secrets, so don't hang around with someone who talks too much"* (Proverbs 20:19).

The second reason is that I want to please God, and God hates gossip. He has given us this command: *"Do not spread slanderous gossip among your people"* (Leviticus 19:16). God's definition of gossip, like His definitions of adultery and murder, has just as much to do with what's going on inside of us as it does with what's observed and overheard by the people around us. Internal gossip—an inward running conversation we have with ourselves about someone we dislike—can do as much damage to a relationship as the external, spoken kind. The subject of my internal tirades may never know how many gigabytes of memory she has occupied in my brain, but she will feel the inevitable result: an unmistakable decline in the quality of our relationship. (Not to mention the fact that God always knows what I'm thinking.) One way or another, what's inside comes out. Jesus said the same thing: *"A good person produces good deeds from a good heart, and an evil person produces evil deeds from an evil heart. Whatever is in your heart determines what you say"* (Luke 6:45).

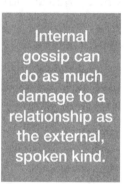

Internal gossip can do as much damage to a relationship as the external, spoken kind.

My sister's husband once went on a business trip with several associates. During the course of their travels, one of his associates, a woman, discovered and purchased some hand cream that smelled absolutely wonderful. Every time she applied the cream, everyone around her sniffed and sighed in ecstasy. So, all of the men on the trip, my brother-in-law included, tracked down the name of the cream, bought some, and brought it home for their wives. My sister really enjoys her fragrant souvenir, and every time I'm with her and she applies it, I grab her hand and hold it to my nose. The stuff smells that good.

Proverbs 27:9 says, "*The heartfelt counsel of a friend is as sweet as perfume.*" I want to have a friend, and I want to be a friend, who is so filled with good stuff on the inside that when pressure is applied, what spills out is good, with a fragrance that blesses everyone in the room.

But what do you do when a friend wants to spill gossip instead? How do you respond without sounding superior or judgmental? One strategy is to make it about you, not about her. Instead of saying, "You shouldn't be gossiping, you know," say something like, "It isn't good for me to hear this. I have enough trouble keeping my own heart right without worrying about someone else's."

Another effective tool for the times when gossip rears its ugly head is to answer every negative statement about the verbal victim with a positive one. Even if you agree with the negative statement, there is almost always something positive that you can say instead of affirming it.

"Have you noticed how much weight Judy has gained lately?" So it begins. A possible response: "She is such a fabulous cook. Have you ever tried one of her Mexican dishes?" Another attempt is made to draw you in: "No, but obviously she has eaten more than her share." Response: "She is so great to have at a party. I love her sense of humor."

If your conversation partner is even moderately intelligent, she will realize that you aren't willing to play her game. Eventually, you may even gain a reputation as someone who is not "safe" to engage in defamatory banter. In this case, it's a good thing to be "unsafe" in a relationship!

Discontentment

Discontentment is another deadly relational toxin. A discontented person is always unhappy about something and easily finds fault with just about anything.

When my husband and I were first married, we relocated to a different city in order to further his career, leaving behind a church that we loved. Naturally, once we'd settled in our new community, we went looking for a church just like the one we'd loved and left. As you might expect, we never found one. We did finally choose a church, much smaller than our previous congregation, where we thought we would feel at home.

My husband was passionate about youth ministry, and I about music, so it was into these two areas that we poured all our energy and enthusiasm. Both areas of ministry happened to fall under the leadership of one pastor who was young and inexperienced, just like us. Having come from a large church teeming with life, we were accustomed to a high standard of excellence. It wasn't long before we grew discontented with the way things were being done in our new church. We could identify ways to improve so much of what they were doing, but we couldn't seem to get the pastor responsible to "catch the vision."

We were aware of others in our circle of church friends who were also frustrated, and our discontentment with the leadership of this young pastor became a frequent topic of conversation when we got together. Somewhere along the line, I had the brilliant idea that those of us who shared this constant diet of complaint should meet together for a banquet of whining and commiseration. I phoned around to invite those I thought would have something to contribute, even managing to suck the senior pastor into our vortex of negativity.

Next on my list to invite was a friend named Marilyn. Thank God for Marilyn—someone who hadn't lost her mind in the sandstorm of groupthink. She said, "No, I won't come to your meeting. This kind of meeting is wrong, and I will have no part in what you are trying to do." She was right. What we were doing was wrong, for about a dozen reasons, not the least of which is the protocol spelled out for us in Matthew 18:15–17, which we will be looking into later.

I am deeply ashamed about having had a part in this ugly scene. Maturity and the School of Hard Knocks have humbled my husband and me over time, and both God and this dear pastor have forgiven us. But I know that, for a time, I was like a contaminated spring, spreading the poison of discontent in that church. That's not something you want on your résumé.

> A person who honors God feels contentment when she looks in the mirror and discontentment when she looks out the window.

Marilyn was right to confront me. I was not a good friend, to the young pastor or to the people I invited to my pity party. Whether our discontentment is related to church leadership, life circumstances, personal finances, or something else, it is always toxic to friendship.

What we focus our attention on, good or bad, begins to take over our lives and then spreads, affecting (or infecting) the lives of others. Do you want to be influenced by someone who obsesses about her dining room décor or about feeding the poor? About the wrinkles on her face or the people on her heart? A person who honors God feels contentment when she looks in the mirror and discontentment when she looks out the window.

Unfortunately, contentment doesn't come automatically, even when we get what we want. Discontentment is an aggressive cancer that is never satisfied. That is why it is critical that we model the apostle Paul's example and learn to be content in all circumstances. His secret? Reliance on God:

> *I have learned to be content whatever the circumstances. I know what it is to be in need, and I know what it is to have plenty. I have learned the secret of being content in any and every situation, whether well fed or hungry, whether living in plenty or in want. I can do everything through him who gives me strength.* (Philippians 4:11–13 NIV)

One of my favorite quotes goes something like this: "Do you live for heaven, or do you live demanding that your life be like heaven? Your response will determine what you'll spend your life fighting for." Choose contentment, and befriend others who embrace it.

Narcissism

A third lethal relational toxin is narcissism. In using this term, I'm not referring to the personality disorder, but rather to what the dictionary defines as "exceptional interest in or admiration for oneself." In other words, "It's all about me."

Any mother can attest to the fact that little children are complete narcissists. Some people call babies little bundles of love.

Wrong! I adore babies, but let's be honest: they are little bundles of selfishness. When they are hungry, they want to be fed—now! It doesn't matter if it's five o'clock in the morning and you've been up all night tending to two sick kids taking turns projectile vomiting every hour, on the hour. Your baby doesn't care. She is hungry, and it's all about her. I know God had good reason for creating children this way. And I also know He intends for us to outgrow this type of behavior, somewhere along the line.

The trouble is, some of us don't. Some people go through life believing that everyone else exists to meet their needs, help them accomplish their goals, and make them happy. This attitude is expressed in dozens of ways in a relationship. A narcissist may manifest this tendency in a minor fashion, such as forgetting a dinner date or always showing up late, or in a major way, such as abandoning one's spouse and children and offering the excuse "I wasn't happy." Usually it is an avalanche of small, disrespectful acts that kill a friendship over time. Regardless of the specifics, the underlying attitude is always, "It's all about me."

A woman ruled by narcissism might say something like this: "You don't mind taking my kids again today, do you? I know you've had them every day this week, but since you don't work, and I do, I thought you could do it." (As if stay-at-home moms don't work.) She assumes that her agenda and her needs are more important than yours. Her treatment of you involves manipulation through guilt, and it communicates disrespect.

Narcissism can manifest in other forms, as well. Take the chronically needy friend who is more interested in occupying your attention than resolving her problems. She wants more than your help. She wants your life. Or the controller who, when you refuse to run your life her way, punishes you either with the heat of her temper or the chill of her distance. She insists that you should do this and you shouldn't do that.

Don't let anyone "should" on you! Submit your relationships to a reality check to see whether you have been bending to any manipulation. Then, replace the word "should" with the words "I choose to," and you will work toward reclaiming your share of the balance of power. You rarely have to walk away from a narcissist. As soon as you establish healthy, nonnegotiable boundaries, she will likely walk away from you, nursing her self-inflicted wounds and playing the victim.

> Submit your relationships to a reality check to see whether you have been bending to any manipulation.

Authors and psychologists John Townsend and Henry Cloud have written several books on boundaries, which I highly recommend reading if you find yourself in relationship with someone who is self-absorbed. The strategies these authors share will help you to deal with this person in a loving but decisive way, for your benefit and hers. The only way a narcissist will grow up to experience loving relationships is if her selfish patterns of behavior no longer succeed in getting her what she wants. Subtlety will not work. If you are in a relationship with a friend who's a "vampire," sucking the life out of you, you are simply a tool.

Evaluating Relational Health

Late missionary and hymn writer Amy Carmichael said, "If I take offence easily, if I am content to continue in cool unfriendliness, though friendship be possible, then I know nothing of Calvary love." So, where do we go from here? How do we know if true friendship is possible? Is there some diagnostic tool that we can use to analyze our friendships and determine whether their toxins can be flushed out of the system or whether the cost of continuing the friendship will be just too great?

I'd like to advance two questions to ask yourself when attempting to answer the above question. These questions are not scientific, by any means, but they will point you in the right direction.

Diagnostic Question #1: Is my friend directionally challenged?

Patty once attended a huge conference in the sports stadium of a major American city. There were thousands and thousands of women in attendance. Everything took a long time. She had to wait to buy food at a concession stand and then wait in line for the restroom. But the greatest challenge and frustration by far was waiting for ten thousand women to navigate their cars out of the stadium parking lot. Some independent but directionally challenged woman would head in the wrong direction, and two thousand others would meekly follow. It was a parking attendant's worst nightmare.

> We must always be aware of the influence our friends have on our relationship with God, whether they call themselves Christians or not.

In a friendship, following the wrong person has far more serious consequences than a traffic jam. An important question to ask ourselves is, "Does the influence of this friend lead me toward God or away from Him?" In his book *Quality Friendship*, Gary Inrig makes this powerful statement: "People are not morally neutral. They either influence our lives for good or for evil. They help us become what they are."[3]

Dr. Inrig is not suggesting that we should sever all ties with people who don't share our spiritual beliefs. Usually, it is through a series of friendships and acquaintances with Christians that unbelieving or spiritually ambivalent people come to faith in Jesus. However, we must always be aware of the influence our friends have on our relationship with God, whether they call themselves Christians or not.

Diagnostic Test #2: Is my friend teachable?

We have already established the importance of two-way accountability in close relationships. If we consider ourselves free to speak truth into the life of a friend, we also must be open to hearing the truth from her. That being said, if our friend is confronted with the truth about her toxic behavior, will she listen openly and receive the message as coming from someone who cares about her? Will she at least seek to understand? Is she teachable, or is she what the book of Proverbs would label a fool? If she can't receive truth that is offered in love and humility, she is not friendship material. Some people just aren't. And if we find ourselves faced with an unteachable person who refuses to change, there is nothing left to do but walk away.

When You Have to Walk Away

Even at this sad moment near the end of the story of a friendship, we can write the last chapter with love and respect. Jean Shaw, in her book *Greater Love*, has come up with a

3. Gary Inrig, *Quality Friendship: The Risks and Rewards* (Chicago: Moody Press, 1981), 126.

creative acronym that is helpful under these difficult circumstances.[4] The letters of this acronym form the word *peace*. As Christians, we should always make peace our goal. The apostle Paul encouraged us, *"Do your part to live in peace with everyone, as much as possible"* (Romans 12:18).

Here is the acronym for *peace*:

Pray for our friend and ourselves.
Explain our position.
Act out of love.
Continue to be kind.
Enlist the help of Christian friends.

Pray

First, we pray. God can change even the most stubborn of hearts. As we approach a friend with the intention of speaking the truth in love, we need to pray that we will do so with pure motives and in a spirit of gentleness and humility. We should also pray that God will open our eyes to see the situation from His perspective and that the words we speak will come from Him. We need to pray that God will soften the heart of our friend and help her to receive our perspective without becoming defensive or argumentative.

Explain

Second, we explain why we no longer wish to continue in the relationship. No excuses, no justification, just the truth. Telling the truth is the greatest kindness we can offer at this bend in the road because only the truth will set us both free to heal and grow. This act of closure is important. When a romance ends, we say

---

4. See Jean Shaw, *Greater Love: Woman's Workshop on Friendship* (Grand Rapids: Zondervan, 1984).

that one lover "broke up" with the other. Often, in friendship, we fail to extend this courtesy. As a result, the discarded friend spends months, even years, wondering why the other person doesn't call her anymore.

Act

Third, we act out of love. If we cannot help but speak in anger or with the intent to punish our former friend, then we are not ready to say anything at all. We need to wait until the intensity of our emotions has diminished. We know that we are ready to act out of love when we regret that the words we need to say will inevitably wound the hearer. If this sense of regret is absent, we know that our motives are not right, and we must return to the first step of prayer.

When we have spoken our piece and ended the friendship, we should not make a point of avoiding the person at all costs or giving her the silent treatment. We must continue to show kindness if we happen to bump into her in casual company or when our circumstances make it impossible to keep our distance—if this person is a coworker or a neighbor, for example. By continuing to extend common courtesy, we communicate respect. This type of behavior says, "I don't choose you as my friend, but I value you as a person created in God's image." We can remove someone from our intimate circle without kicking her out of our lives entirely. Only in the rare case when a former friend is abusive is it necessary to avoid all contact.

Enlist

Finally, we must enlist the support of our true friends. For some, their only true friend is a family member or maybe God. No matter who makes up our intimate circle, we must allow them to help us heal and grow. We should use the lessons learned from the pain of a toxic friendship to make us wise, and we ought to address any issues in our hearts that the conflict may have brought to light. That way, we will be prepared when God gives us another chance at friendship.

There is no sin, no shame, in creating distance between yourself and someone who has set a precedent for relational damage. David did it. When King Saul pursued him with the intent to harm him—and, later, when David's own son Absalom did the same thing—David fled. The challenge in these situations is walking away without taking any emotional baggage with you. And you're in luck, because that's our next topic of discussion.

TOXIC FRIENDSHIPS

Questions for Reflection and Discussion

1. In what ways have you seen envy affect friendship?

2. Have you ever experienced a friend's behavior shining a spotlight on something about yourself that you disliked? How did you respond to that discomfort?

3. Do you struggle with gossip—internal, external, or both? If so, brainstorm some ways of rerouting your thoughts and/or conversations.

4. What do you believe is the secret of contentment? (See Philippians 4:11–13.)

5. Gary Inrig wrote, "People are not morally neutral. They either influence our lives for good or for evil. They help us become what they are." Do you agree? What are your thoughts on your circle of friends in light of that statement?

6. Romans 12:18 says, *"Do your part to live in peace with everyone, as much as possible."* Thinking of the people in your life, have you done your part?

8

MENDING FENCES

One of the uncompromising realities in the world of relationships is that people get hurt. Usually, it isn't that we set out to wound one another, but the truth is that we are all complex creatures. The motives and emotions that drive us are like crosscurrents affecting the course of a raft. They don't always take us where we intended to go. And once the damage is done, we often need a map to get back on track.

I vividly remember the first turbulent season of what had been an almost ripple-free life. The stability I had long taken for granted was at stake. I felt fragile, disappointed, and afraid. My idealism, nurtured by a happy life, lay dying inside me as cold, hard reality hovered expectantly overhead. I was finding out that the people you trust aren't always trustworthy, that Christians don't always act like Christians, and that sometimes the people you thought really loved you really don't.

As hard as it was to accept the betrayal of so many peripheral people in my life, that was nothing compared with the searing grief caused by the infidelity of those I considered true friends.

As the fabric of life, as I knew it, unraveled, creating the worst heartache I had ever known, I began to notice a pronounced aloofness in my two closest friends. They seemed never to have time for me, yet, strangely, seemed to have ample time for each other. Why would they abandon me now, when I needed their support more than ever?

Relational Repair

I needed an answer, and I was too desperate for pride or decorum. I was on the phone with Diane, arranging the details of our fifth annual joint summer vacation. I had assumed that we would continue the tradition, since nothing had been said to the contrary. Then, in very vague terms, Diane said she wasn't sure a vacation with us would work out this year. I immediately knew something was wrong. Our shared vacations had always been the highlight of the year for both couples. We would laugh all year long about the memories we'd made on those adventures. Anticipation of this special time had become one of the few bright spots in my darkening world.

"What's going on?" I demanded. "I need you now! Please, tell me what's wrong!"

Long pause.

"We've got to talk," she said finally.

Diane rearranged her schedule and came over right away. At last, she told to me what she had been discussing with our mutual friend Rita—how I had offended her.

I asked her to forgive me for causing offense, and she asked me the same for taking it to a third party instead of directly to me. We reconciled and began again. That is the goal of restoration—not to "patch up" a relationship so that we can somehow tolerate each other but to recreate the friendship, making it better than it was before.

The English poet Alexander Pope said, "To err is human; to forgive, divine." I know this is true. Someone with my oversensitive, excessively analytical nature doesn't let go of an affront easily. Yet the quality of my friendship with Diane actually improved after this fracture, even though I had been deeply hurt. The improvement was God's doing. We did what we knew how to do, and God did the rest, resulting in a deep healing in our hearts and our relationship.

Through Diane's disclosure, I learned that her aggravation with me had found a receptive ear in Rita because I had offended her in a similar way. I knew what had to come next. I had to confront Rita.

She came over for coffee, and I mustered up the courage to say, "Things have not been right between us. Please tell me what I've done to upset you." At this point, I knew I had done something to upset her, but because Diane and I had taken care not to discuss any details pertaining to Rita, I was unclear as to exactly what that was.

We talked, and the outcome of our conversation was resolution. A few days later, I received a card from Rita that began something like this:

Dear Donna,

Thank you for showing me what a real friend does when there is deep water in a relationship….

Rita had outlived many disappointing friendships, but this was the first time in her experience that anyone had cared enough to stay and do the work needed to repair a rift rather than avoiding the conflict by simply moving on.

Sometimes, you take the risk, you do the work, and still you lose a friend—either immediately, because she will not forgive, or gradually, because she refuses to be real, and so the awkwardness of unresolved conflict lies between you. I have experienced this, as well.

But it doesn't have to be that way. The Bible gives us clear instructions for handling discord in relationships. And I know from experience that when these steps are followed, many times, though not always, the relationships that come out the other side are worth the sacrifice of our pride and the risk to our friendship. Let's explore some of these steps together.

Take the Initiative

In *The Message* translation of the Bible, a passage in Matthew 5 reads like this:

> *If you enter your place of worship and, about to make an offering, you suddenly remember a grudge a friend has against you, abandon your offering, leave immediately, go to this friend and make things right. Then and only then, come back and work things out with God. Or say you're out in the street and an old enemy accosts you. Don't lose a minute. Make the first move; make things right with him.*
> (Matthew 5:23–25 MSG)

Later on in the same gospel account, Matthew records Jesus as saying, *"If a fellow believer hurts you, go and tell him—work it out between the two of you. If he listens, you've made a friend"* (Matthew 18:15 MSG).

Jesus values unbroken relationship above almost anything else, and His meaning here is clear. Whether we hurt someone else or someone else has hurt us, the ball is always in our court. The initiative to repair the damage done to a relationship is always ours to take, even when the responsibility for the damage is not.

When someone has wounded us, we must take the initiative to make things right.

Silently punishing someone who has brought hurt into our lives and waiting for her emotional ESP to kick in and tell her she was wrong may feel gratifying for a time. But indulging the instinct to retaliate this way robs both parties of the potential for closeness.

When someone has wounded us, we must take the initiative to make things right. The same is true on those occasions when we are responsible for the damage. Allowing fear or pride to prevent us from approaching a friend about something we have done to hurt her may also mark an end of the road we travel together.

Still not convinced? Let's see what the Word of God has to say on the subject.

People with good sense restrain their anger; they earn esteem by overlooking wrongs. (Proverbs 19:11)

Be humble and gentle. Be patient with each other, making allowance for each other's faults because of your love. Try always to be led along together by the Holy Spirit and so be at peace with one another. (Ephesians 4:2–3 TLB)

Make every effort to live in peace with all men....
(Hebrews 12:14 NIV)

Most important of all, continue to show deep love for each other, for love covers a multitude of sins. (1 Peter 4:8)

"*Make every effort....*" "*Most important of all....*" The Word of God is pretty serious about relational unity. Many other Scriptures confirm that we are not to be prickly, perpetually offended people. There are times when the Holy Spirit enables us to cut a friend some slack by overlooking an offense and forgiving her in our hearts without the closure of confrontation.

Other times, we can't simply overlook a wrong that was committed against us. Forgive, yes; overlook, no. It's too big. Our hearts won't let us. Maybe it's because we fear that the offense will be repeated, or because it is causing us harm that cannot be righted by our willingness to forgive. Or maybe it's because our friend needs to grow by learning to relate in a more positive way. Sometimes, we have to confront someone in order for the friendship to continue. The Bible neither skirts nor condemns this reality. Rather, it gives us steps to follow so that we may create maximum opportunity for growth and minimum room for harm.

Find the Courage to Confront

The goal of a confrontation is not to win a battle; it is to win back a friend. Anyone who proceeds without reconciliation as her objective may get a load off her chest, but she will only escalate the conflict and eliminate the friendship.

In His Sermon on the Mount, Jesus sounded a warning about confrontation when He said the following:

Stop judging others, and you will not be judged. For others will treat you as you treat them. Whatever measure you use in judging others, it will be used to measure how you are judged. And why worry about a speck in your friend's eye when you have a log in your own? How can you think of saying, "Let me help you get rid of that speck in your eye," when you can't see past the log in your own eye? Hypocrite! First get rid of the log from your own eye; then perhaps you will see well enough to deal with the speck in your friend's eye. (Matthew 7:1–5)

Confronting a friend must be done very, very carefully. First, we must ensure that we are not "visually impaired" ourselves. If there is a log in our own eye—some sin or offensive behavior we have not yet dealt with or apologized for—the chances are good that the speck obstructing our friend's ability to see her error is a splinter from the same piece of wood that's blinding us. Keeping this in mind, we should humble ourselves and ask God to reveal the condition of our own hearts before we approach someone else about the condition of hers.

> We should humble ourselves and ask God to reveal the condition of our own hearts before we approach someone else about the condition of hers.

Second, we must conduct ourselves with gentleness, as tenderly as a mother would extract a sliver of wood from the eye of her child. We must do our best to avoid causing further injury or unnecessary pain.

Within weeks of settling in the Fraser Valley, before I had made a single friend, I was asked by those in our church's leadership to teach a women's Bible study. I was excited about the opportunity to teach and the potential for connecting with other women. I worked hard to prepare each lesson, week by week, and I felt that the sessions had been going well.

My bubble was about to burst. Only a few weeks into the fall term, I received a letter from one of the women who had been participating in my study. Her letter outlined all of the things I was doing wrong as a Bible study leader. At the end of the long list of blunt, often personal, critiques, my correspondent assured me that she didn't intend to hurt me, just to help me improve my teaching style.

Let me tell you, I found nothing helpful in that letter. Reading it left me feeling angry, hurt, and defensive. It was clear to me that it had been written with the intent to harm, and clearer still was that it needed a response. Still, I knew I couldn't trust my heart to weigh the validity of her criticism or to craft a civil reply.

So, I took the letter, my hurt feelings, and my damaged pride before God. I prayed over every accusation on the list until I had written down a gentle response to each one. In regard to some of this woman's "concerns," I had questions. I wanted her to clarify her meaning. For other concerns, I offered a brief explanation as to why I had chosen the methods I had been using. Still other items on the list required an apology from me. Although I had not done anything malicious, I may have lacked sensitivity in certain areas.

The ensuing confrontation with the woman on the other end of the bitter pen was almost certainly not what she had expected. I called her on the phone, and as I spoke to her, I made no attempts to defend myself. I simply addressed each item on her list with the calmness and composure God had given me. I couldn't really deal with whatever unhealthy emotions had spawned her ink-and-paper assault, because her letter had explicitly denied their existence.

This woman continued to attend the study, but I didn't hear another word from her until a few months later. She came to me not with words of criticism but with a confession. Yes, she admitted, she had meant for her letter to hurt me. But my lack of a blustery response had taken all the wind out of her sails and allowed her to see her heart as it truly was.

Not every confrontation has such a happy ending. But the Bible gives us a protocol to follow for those, as well. If our private discussions fail to bring resolution with another Christ follower, we are to go to someone else within our Christian community and solicit mediation. We have the following instructions from Jesus Himself:

> If another believer sins against you, go privately and point out the fault. If the other person listens and confesses it, you have won that person back. But if you are unsuccessful, take one or two others with you and go back again, so that everything you say may be confirmed by two or three witnesses.
>
> (Matthew 18:15–16)

Look for someone in your church or in the greater Christian community—someone with the moral authority to bring an objective, biblical perspective to the situation. A person with moral authority is one who is widely respected, not necessarily because he or she occupies a position of leadership but because of a track record of quality character, behavior, and decision making. Once you have solicited the help of such an individual, agree to accept his or her compassionate, unbiased resolution, and then work toward making peace.

Our mandate is to be peacemakers, not peacekeepers. Keeping peace often involves shoveling unhealed wounds and unkind words under the carpet, where they accumulate, coagulate, and propagate. Making peace, on the other hand, sometimes involves confrontation, but confrontation always involves forgiveness.

Summon the Grace to Forgive

In an earlier chapter, and previously in this chapter, I alluded to a deep wound that occurred in connection with my husband's employment at a church. Unfortunately, the most painful experiences of my life have centered on churches—strange words from someone who travels around speaking about finding faith, I know. "Come to church. Nearly killed me, but you'll love it. Really!"

But every church is like a family. And, like a family, every church is, to some degree, dysfunctional. Church members hurt one another, just as family members do. But we don't give up on the family because it hurts too much. I haven't given up on church, either. In fact, I love my church. When the winter winds start to blow in this frosty part of the world, and the mercury plunges so low that we can't even read the thermometer, my church and my family are about the only things that keep me here in the great, white north.

I must admit, though, that there was a time when I came close to giving up on the church. I wanted to "home-church" my kids. But I also wanted to be free of the anger, pain, and bitterness that loomed like a menacing black cloud over our home. To do that, I knew I needed to forgive those whom I felt had wronged my family and me.

I learned that forgiveness is a path we must choose to take. Walking that path involves a decision to begin traveling in the right direction—and many subsequent choices to remain on that path until we've reached the end. And we know we've reached the end when we get there.

There were many landmarks along my path to forgiveness, and one of the first I remember was receiving a long-distance phone call to our new home in the Fraser Valley from one of the leaders of our former church home. This man had been a friend and coworker before the meltdown that had propelled us away from all that was familiar.

I answered the phone, and the sound of this man's voice produced an immediate reaction. I began to shake uncontrollably, and a knot formed in my stomach that felt about the size of Texas. It was obvious that this man still had incredible power over me—and that I would never be free from his sway until I had forgiven him.

In my quiet times with God, I would work through the various scenes from our conflict and ask Him to help me sort out my emotions and show me where my sin lay. As I worked hard toward healing, I discovered some valuable truths—namely, that time alone won't heal a broken heart, and the healing process cannot be rushed. It can be slowed down and delayed if you do not cooperate with God, but it cannot be sped up; there is no "fast track" to healing.

Several times during this process, I thought that I could see the end of the path, but then someone or something else would come to mind, and I would have to forgive that person or confess and repent of my bitter resentment, whether it had

> The healing process can be slowed down and delayed if you do not cooperate with God, but it cannot be sped up.

been directed at a person or at God. With each of these steps came the pain of peeling another layer of callus away from my heart.

You see, we are never completely the victim. Out of our pains come sinful attitudes and behaviors aimed at protecting ourselves from future mistreatment.

Dr. Larry Crabb made an insightful point along these lines in his book *Inside Out*:

> Certainly we struggle as victims of other people's unkindness. We have been sinned against. But we cannot excuse our sinful responses to others on the grounds of their mistreatment of us. We are responsible for what we do. We are both strugglers and sinners, victims and agents, people who hurt and people who harm.[5]

In retrospect, it's apparent to me how, with gentleness and wisdom, God brought to the surface some issues that needed my attention. In His timing, He prepared me for each issue and gave me the grace to do what He required of me: recall the hurt, feel the pain, and forgive anyway.

You have probably heard the phrase "forgive and forget." Some people believe that forgiving and forgetting are one and the same. But forgetting isn't forgiveness; it's denial. To forgive, we must recall the hurt. That's the easy part. Then, we must feel the pain—because unless we really own the injury, with our emotions engaged, any forgiveness we presume to offer is not real, and it won't bring the release and healing that result from genuine forgiveness.

As your mind goes to some hurtful scene in your past, your heart may be crying out, "It isn't fair! What about justice?" You

---

5. Larry Crabb, *Inside Out* [expanded 10th anniversary edition] (Colorado Springs: NavPress, 1988), 126.

might want to demand that your adversary pay for the wrongs he or she has committed against you. But Jesus has already paid for them. He paid for your sins and mine; the sins of your friends and mine; the sins of your enemies and mine.

> *It was our weaknesses he carried; it was our sorrows that weighed him down....He was wounded and crushed for our sins. He was beaten that we might have peace. He was whipped, and we were healed! All of us have strayed away like sheep. We have left God's paths to follow our own. Yet the LORD laid on him the guilt and sins of us all.*
>
> (Isaiah 53:4–6)

Where is the justice? The justice is found in the cross of Christ. Jesus paid the price for all sin and suffering with His own blood.

Don't wait until you feel like forgiving someone who has wounded you. More than likely, you will never reach that point. Instead, decide to forgive. Do it for your own sake. Do it to break free from the pain of the past.

In her book *Adventures in Prayer*, the late Catherine Marshall likens the act of forgiveness to the turning of a large ship. The rudder, though a tiny part of the ship, has the power to turn the entire vessel around, given time. The rudder is like our will, Marshall says. And if we are faithful to set the rudder of our will toward forgiveness, then, in time, God will turn the whole person, including our emotions, around to face the same direction. Forgiveness is all about the will.

First, we must engage our will and make a decision to forgive. This step does not necessarily entail speaking to the offending person and telling her that we've forgiven her. In some cases, depending on the state of the offending party's emotional health, telling her "I forgive you" makes the situation worse. So, first, we tell God. We say, "Lord, I choose to forgive my friend, even though her actions have made me feel _____ (rejected/ embarrassed/etc.)."

Second, we decide to walk the path to forgiveness. That means that, every time we're reminded of our wounds and the individual who wounded us, whether it's from hearing about her or seeing her in person, we reaffirm our choice to forgive her. We go to God and say, "I choose to walk in forgiveness today." And we make this choice, again and again, until, one day, we no longer need to, because the forgiveness is complete.

When we are walking the path to forgiveness, it is obvious when we have reached the end. For me, the path to forgiveness ended at a wedding. As we pulled into the parking lot of the church where I had been so deeply wounded, I remembered thinking, *I'll never darken the door of that church again.* Yet, here I was, only a few years later, free of pain, free of anger, and feeling so blessed—blessed because, through God's grace alone, I had managed to move on; I was no longer bitter but better. I had developed a closer intimacy with Jesus, a keener awareness of my own needs and others'. I was better able to be real with people, leaving the matter of my reputation to God. And I was better able to trust Him to work out every circumstance for my ultimate good.

> *Since God chose you to be the holy people whom he loves, you must clothe yourselves with tenderhearted mercy, kindness, humility, gentleness, and patience. You must make allowance for each other's faults and forgive the person who offends you. Remember, the Lord forgave you, so you must forgive others. And the most important piece of clothing you must wear is love. Love is what binds us all together in perfect harmony.*
> (Colossians 3:12–14)

Forgiveness frees us to rebuild a damaged relationship. It's a turning of the page; a rebooting of the computer. Both Randy and I have been invited back to speak several times at the church where we had experienced so much pain. Today, we can walk into that building with healed hearts—and without experiencing the slightest discomfort in conversing with anyone we might

Forgiveness frees us to rebuild a damaged relationship.

meet there. Even more beautiful, God has reconnected our hearts with that place and the people there, something He alone could have done.

Surrender Your Expectations

Virtually all conflict and stress in life comes as a result of your expectations. You expected your husband to come home from work on time so that he could watch the kids while you ran to the store before it closed. You expected to have your house paid off by now. You expected to outlive your children. You expected to have children. You expected your friend to be faithful.

You didn't expect to get laid off. You didn't expect to have car trouble on the highway. You didn't expect to be obligated to reenter the workforce at this stage in life. And now, you are angry and frustrated, stressed and afraid. Your expectations have collided with reality, and you have to decide how to deal with the damage.

I was born with a minor but weird abnormality that causes all my body tissues to be unusually elastic. This has its advantages: for example, I never had any stretch marks from my pregnancies. However, during pregnancy, I could barely take a step without having one joint or another collapse. So, yes, elastic body tissue has some definite disadvantages, including kneecaps that dislocate at will, flat feet, and a jaw that clicks. By the time I retire, I fully expect that I'll be held together with baling wire.

Many years ago, when my husband was a youth pastor, I was playing baseball with the youth group one afternoon when, miraculously, I orchestrated contact between the bat in my hands and the ball hurtling toward me. This had me rushing around the bases as fast as my jellylike joints would carry me. Unfortunately, somewhere between third base and home plate, my left kneecap went AWOL.

This is always painful, but it has the potential to cause significant injury if I am traveling at a high speed. When I hit the ground, which is bound to happen when your foot comes down hard and the knee of the same leg dislocates, the pain was so intense that I couldn't breathe. Compared to the pain of this trauma, breathing through labor contractions was a piece of cake. Unfortunately, at this point in life, I had yet to undergo any training in prenatal breathing.

After being treated at the hospital and then released with all the appropriate bandages, braces, and crutches, I took up residence on the couch of our two-story home. I was stuck there at all times, unless someone was available to help me relocate. I couldn't even use the bathroom on my own.

If you've ever had a joint injury, you have a rare understanding of just how connected everything is in your body. I mean, I couldn't move an eyelash without its affecting my damaged joint. Despite the heavy painkillers I was on, every movement was a new adventure in pain.

Randy did his best to look after me. Yet, while my activities were on hold until further notice, he still had a life. The day after the accident, he had to leave the house, so he called one of my close friends, told her about my condition, and asked if she could come over to help me. She said yes, and Randy left with the confidence that I would be in good hands.

But she never came. I lay on the couch all day, looking forward to her company, looking forward to having something to eat, and looking forward to going to the bathroom. With every hour that passed, the sorrier for myself I felt, and the more hurt, disappointed, and angry I became. "She'd better have a good excuse," I fumed. "How dare she let me down?"

As it turned out, she didn't have a very good excuse. She was just enjoying what she was doing too much to be interrupted. I guess she didn't understand how badly I needed her that day. Of course, I had every reason to feel disappointed.

As women, we often find ourselves in this type of situation. We care deeply, and so we expect others to feel the same. We nurture and want to be nurtured in return. We tend to expect others to know what we want from them, even if we've never expressed it to them, and then we grow angry when they fail to read our minds.

It's okay to make our needs and wants clear. It's okay to tell our friends when they have disappointed us. It's even alright to walk away from a friendship with someone who perpetually disappoints us. But we have no right to demand that our friends meet our expectations. Any effort on our part to coerce someone to do what we want is a manipulative, relationally toxic move.

> It's okay to make our needs and wants clear. But we have no right to demand that our friends meet our expectations.

In the novel *The Shack*, author William Young explains the difference between expectation and expectancy.[6] How many of us build up huge expectations for Christmas each year? You want, you expect, everything to be perfect. Then, your kids get the flu, or your husband gives you an electric grill pan instead of the shimmering negligee you expected, or the bird you roast comes out as dry as turkey jerky. And you are devastated. It was supposed to be perfect, and it's not. Your hopes are shattered, all because your expectations fell far short of reality. Expectation demands, while expectancy delights. Expectancy enables you to swallow your disappointments and find the good in the situation. At least the house is quiet (with the kids sick in bed), and you can grill up some pork chops in your new frying pan for Christmas dinner!

Okay, those were poor examples. But at least you can see the benefits of expectancy versus expectation. Expectancy in a relationship means that I can approach spending time with my friend feeling hopeful that it will be fun and special, yet refraining from defining what that will look like or demanding that she live up to my expectations. Instead of establishing specific criteria my friend must meet in order for our get-together to qualify as satisfying and worthwhile, I can instead anticipate good things *in general* without envisioning them, counting on them, and then becoming bitter when my vision is not fulfilled.

The apostle James discussed what happens when we cling with iron fists to our expectations:

> *Where do you think all these appalling wars and quarrels come from? Do you think they just happen? Think again. They come about because you want your own way, and fight for it deep inside yourselves. You lust for what you don't have*

6. See William P. Young, *The Shack* (Los Angeles: Windblown Media, 2007), 204–206.

*and are willing to kill to get it. You want what isn't yours
and will risk violence to get your hands on it.*

(James 4:1–2 MSG)

When our friends disappoint us, the natural response is to
fret and fume. We can rail and rage against the people we love the
most—and then watch our relationships founder in the after-
shocks. Or, we can surrender our expectations to God. That way,
we can move forward, sometimes disappointed but not angry.
We may be sad but not stressed, knowing that people are flawed
and fickle but God is not. Only the person who is learning to
surrender her expectations to God knows how often He uses
the collision between our expectations and reality to reach out
to us, redirect us, and remind us of His absolute, unwavering
faithfulness.

We can't manage our relationships our own way, with no
regard for God, and expect Him to bless them. He formed our
hearts, and He knows how they work. But we can honor God
and invite His presence and blessing into our friendships as we
take the initiative to be peacemakers and as we confront lovingly,
forgive liberally, and surrender our expectations to Him.

MENDING FENCES

Questions for Reflection and Discussion

1. Think of a time when a friend wounded you in some way. Did you confront your friend? Did you just allow the friendship to slip away? How do you feel about that decision now?

2. Why is it so important that we pray for discernment before we confront someone? Matthew 7:3–5 provides one reason, but there are more.

3. Have you ever approached conflict resolution using the steps laid out in Matthew 18:15–17? If so, what was the result? If not, why do you think you were reluctant to follow these steps?

4. Reread the quote from Dr. Larry Crabb: "Certainly we struggle as victims of other people's unkindness. We have been sinned against. But we cannot excuse our sinful responses to others on the grounds of their mistreatment of us. We are responsible for what we do. We are both strugglers and sinners, victims and agents, people who hurt and people who

harm." What are some evidences from your own experience of the truth of these statements?

5. How is it possible for justice to be served if the person who offended us never pays for what was done? (See Isaiah 53:4–6.)

6. In what ways might your friendships improve if you started employing God's guidelines for relationship management?

Part IV

THE PRIVILEGE OF FRIENDSHIP

9

WHEN YOU CAN'T FIND A FRIEND

When I was eight years old, my dad was recruited from his job in Regina, a mid-sized city on the prairies, to Calgary, a much larger city, with a view of the Rockies, that was the epicenter of the burgeoning Canadian oil industry.

We moved to Calgary in the summertime, weeks away from the start of school, and so there was no natural fishing pool for friends. One day, Dad came home from work and said to me, "See that blue house down the street? I met a man at work today who lives there, and he has a daughter about your age."

That was all it took. I marched down the street, rang the doorbell, and said, "I heard you have a little girl about my age. Can she come out to play?" She did. We played, and before I even knew that her name was Karen, I had found a friend. If only it were that easy for adults.

Maybe you are someone who has always struggled with friendships. It could be that, in the course of reading this book, the light has come on and you have begun to understand why. Perhaps you have identified toxic tendencies in yourself. Maybe a fear of confrontation has kept you from entering the emotional "danger zone" that exists on the road to every relationship that has weathered its storms and stood the test of time. Maybe you've grown quite comfortable wearing a mask, and you can't bear to think of removing it. Or perhaps you've realized that you need to work on one or more of the essential traits of a true friend.

It may be that you've recently made a transition that required you to leave everyone you love behind, and you wonder if, in this season of life, you will ever connect with anyone else on the heart level.

What you need now are tools to cultivate the soil of your heart and prepare it to receive the seeds of future friendships.

Strategies for Finding a Friend

Many lonely people who are longing for a friend don't know how to take the steps needed to find one—or be one. It's as if they hope to trip over the perfect friend on the way to the office. Sometimes, the problem is that they are not tuned in socially. If that's the case, even if they did trip over the "perfect friend," they would probably just regain their footing and move on.

My sister was having trouble getting her husband to remember to take out the trash. Instead of doing it herself or nagging him about it, she positioned the garbage bag in front of the door he used every day when leaving for work. Somehow, this competent, well-educated, otherwise high-functioning man managed to move the garbage bag out of the way, open the door, and leave for work without taking the trash to the curb. I kid you not. He wasn't simply being stubborn or displaying passive-aggressive behavior; he just wasn't tuned in.

Getting tuned in to our relationships means taking a close look in several places: inward, to evaluate whether we are quality friendship material; outward, to see who is available for friendship right now; and upward, to ask God to bring someone new into our lives and/or to open our eyes to see the potential for friendship.

Be Someone

Before you can love another person, you have to love yourself; and before you can be someone's friend, you have to be someone yourself. You need to know who you are and what you have to offer in a relationship.

> Before you can be someone's friend, you have to be someone yourself. You need to know who you are and what you have to offer in a relationship.

Denise emerged from a pretty traumatic childhood without a distinct personality of her own. She had traded her individuality for emotional survival and had mastered the art of character camouflage, so that she was defined by the character of the person she was with at any given time. If she found herself in the company of someone who liked Chinese food, then she, too, liked Chinese food. If she went shopping with someone who loved pink, then she came home with bags full of pink clothing. If her boyfriend wanted her to have sex with him, the word *no* never crossed her lips, even though her heart was screaming it. Because her own opinions had never been sought or valued, she made her decisions based on what would please everyone else, what would incur the fewest unpleasant consequences, and what would earn her acceptance at that moment.

But Denise was desperately lonely. Although caving in and catering to the desires of others gained her momentary acceptance, it never brought her the intimacy she desired. This is because, again, before you can be someone's friend, you have to be someone. But how do you become somebody when the entirety of your life experience has taught you that you are a "nobody"?

We tend to think of value as a subjective thing. What is valued by one person is discarded as worthless by another.

When Celine Dion launched her "Let's Talk about Love" tour, she invited a group of children to perform the title track with her at every concert venue, just as had been done on the CD recording. Our daughter Kendall was one of about twenty kids selected for this privilege at the concert in Calgary, and we were thrilled for her. What an opportunity!

There was just one problem: all the tickets for the concert were snatched up before we even found out that Kendall had been chosen to participate. We did everything short of selling our souls to find tickets. It didn't matter to us if they were lousy seats; we would have been happy sitting backstage, in the nosebleed section, anywhere within earshot. Randy and I kept our ears glued to the radio and dived like mad for the phone whenever an opportunity to win tickets was announced.

But it was not to be. The night of the concert, I sat at home, feeling sorry for myself and wishing I could see my little girl's radiant face as she confidently belted out the song she had worked so hard to perfect, according to "Celine standard."

A few days later, I found out that the mother of a friend of mine had been given tickets to the concert but had decided not to go. She hadn't sold the tickets or even given them away, because she hadn't realized their potential value to others like me. Instead, she'd let them go to waste. She wasn't a big fan of Celine Dion, I guess. And her daughter wasn't launching a vocal career. To that woman, those little strips of printed cardstock weren't worth very much.

In certain cases, value is relative. But not when it comes to people. To God, human beings are priceless. And that's just the good news. The great news is that He is right—about your worth, about my worth, about everything. Jesus doesn't just know the truth; He *is* the truth. (See John 14:6.) And He proved that each of us is of inestimable value when He paid the ultimate price—His very life—for the mere possibility of a relationship with us.

Evangelist Joe Aldrich said it this way, in his booklet entitled *Self-worth*:

> If the whole world decided you were worthless, it would not change your essential value. Why? Because as a believer you share both the image and nature of the unchanging God Himself. Your value is tied to Him. He is the magnetic north pole of your essential worth. The Almighty Creator is the infinite reference point, the ultimate standard, the "cosmic blue book" of your value. He made you in His image and likeness. Your value was written in blood at the cross. And whatever He values is valuable.[7]

The first step toward being someone is to understand your value, deep in the core of your soul. The remaining steps are a

7. Joseph C. Aldrich, *Self-worth: How to Become More Loveable* (Portland: Multnomah Press, 1982).

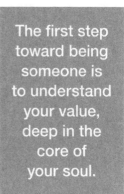

The first step toward being someone is to understand your value, deep in the core of your soul.

process of learning to act like you do—making choices, forming opinions, and recognizing your needs and ideas with the conviction that they really matter because you are a person of dignity and worth.

It took some counseling and a lot of prayer, Bible study, and reflection, but Denise has come to see herself through Jesus' eyes. She loves herself and feels worthy of the love of others. She chooses better friends, and better friends choose her.

Be Proactive

By the time my first Calgarian friend, Karen, and I were ten or so, we had gone our separate ways. She was attending a Roman Catholic school and I a public one. I lost track of her for thirty years. Then, at a city-wide Billy Graham crusade, our paths crossed again. I had been part of the program, and when she saw me onstage, she recognized me immediately. She took the initiative and reintroduced herself, wrapping me in a big hug.

The amazing thing is that our first lunch together after that reunion launched us just as quickly and as deeply into friendship as our first meeting had. Karen is now one of my closest, most respected, and most trusted friends. How sad it would have been if she had not proactively sought me out at that event! Making friends usually requires action. Seldom does God providentially drop a new companion in our lap. We have to take steps to pursue a relationship with a potential friend and then pause to see if she wants to close the gap.

One day, I received an e-mail from Becky, a friend with whom I'd mostly lost contact for many years. But in the weeks prior to my receiving her e-mail, we had seen each other a few times and had shared a couple of good conversations. In her e-mail, she wrote that in the course of seeing me lately, she'd felt a real affinity for me, and she asked whether I could see us becoming more intentional about our friendship. "Yes!" I said out loud to my computer. "I would love that!" The affinity she'd felt was mutual, and I was so glad she had taken the time and the risk to invite me into a deeper level of friendship.

I've extended similar invitations to other women, including Wendy. Wendy is probably the brightest woman I know. I had always admired her for her innate sense of style, her bubbly personality, her sense of humor, and especially the way she had chosen to channel her considerable gifts and intellect to do something significant in the world. Because she occupied a high-profile position of leadership, I was able to observe her and "get to know" her—from a distance—without her really knowing me.

After spending one too many weekends at home with the kids while my husband was away speaking, I decided I needed a single friend. Single, because I felt uncomfortable asking my married friends to take time away from their families just because I was alone. But I was tired of having no social life on the weekends.

I had met Wendy several times and knew she was single, and I wondered whether she and I could become friends. I approached her much the same way I had approached Karen as an eight-year-old: I phoned her and explained that I wanted to get to know her. Would she be interested in having dinner together on the weekend? She said yes, and another wonderful friendship was born.

In retrospect, I realize that it sounds a little like I was asking Wendy out on a date. But the direct, honest approach has always worked for me. You may not be quite as bold, but you can still be proactive in pursuing new friendships.

Catherine is a friend of mine whose husband is an executive in the oil industry. His work has required the family to move often. In the time I've known Catherine, she has been a resident of Texas, Calgary, and Alaska. For her sake, I'm relieved she can't go much further north before heading south again. As a result of these frequent relocations, Catherine has become an expert at making new friends. Some of her strategies include getting involved in her children's schools, where she meets other moms with children around the same age as hers; getting involved at church, which enables her to meet women of similar ministry interests; and joining book clubs through a local bookstore or library. If you are looking for a friend, you have a lot of options. Accept invitations, take classes, join clubs, and get involved. You never know where an important intersection will take place.

If you do nothing else, make sure you pray. Your heavenly Father knows your needs, and He delights in giving good gifts to His children. When we pray passionately for something, our eyes are wide open, looking for the answer to that prayer. But, as we will see, God may have a purpose in isolating us for a period of time. Sometimes, when we are on the hunt for a friendship, we are also avoiding the work He wants to do inside us or in another important relationship, whether with another person or with Him.

The Lessons of Loneliness

After Patty and her husband, Marshall, came to faith, their marriage still struggled for years. Both of them had a whole convoy of baggage that they had accumulated over years of abuse, poor choices, and pain. They had never learned how to relate to each other in a way that would foster intimacy and trust.

Although Patty loved Marshall deeply, she felt it was safer for her to find emotional intimacy in friendship. Her reasoning was that if those relationships were to fail, she would recover, but she wasn't sure that she could survive her husband's rejection. So, she avoided entering the danger zone of allowing herself to be truly known by the one person whose acceptance meant everything to her.

Patty suffered one train wreck of a friendship after another until she finally realized that offering her unmasked heart to Marshall actually posed less of a risk than these other relationships. It had finally become apparent to her that God was not going to let her replace her husband—and the friendship she could have with him—with any other friend. Patty had some casual acquaintances she could 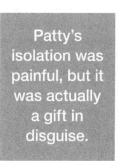 meet for lunch, and she had me, but I was a ten-hour car ride away—close enough to give support and encouragement over the phone or via e-mail, but too far to share her life as Marshall could.

Patty's isolation was painful, but it was actually a gift in disguise. Given the nourishment of time, trust, and necessity, her marriage opened up like a flower unfolding its petals to the sun. As she and Marshall have learned to relax in the security of their unique, one-flesh connection, God has begun gifting them both with quality friendships with other men and women, as well.

God's Friendship Should Be Our First Priority

God, in His kindness, insists that we get our relational priorities straight. During our first year in the Fraser Valley, I languished in loneliness. We had arrived there with our emotional gauges on empty. My husband's response to this condition was to get busy. Mine was to retreat.

Far removed from my support network, my world was reduced to the size of my little family: Kevann, just a baby at the time; Kendall, a preschooler; and Randy, running fast and furious in his efforts to inject life into a listless youth ministry. Never before had I lacked for things to do or people to do them with. Now I was alone. So alone.

It was sheer desperation that drove me into the arms of God. Honestly, if there had been anyone else, I wouldn't have chosen Him. He knew that. And because He wasn't willing to play second fiddle to my other relationships anymore, He allowed me to feel isolated for a time—not to punish me but to show me that He was, and always will be, my best Friend. He has always been there for me, and He always will be. In fact, He said, *"Never will I leave you; never will I forsake you"* (Hebrews 13:5 NIV).

I love the word picture Jesus paints for us in John 15 of the vine and the branches.

> *I am the true vine....Remain in me, and I will remain in you. For a branch cannot produce fruit if it is severed from the vine, and you cannot be fruitful apart from me. Yes, I am the vine; you are the branches. Those who remain in me, and I in them, will produce much fruit. For apart from me you can do nothing. Anyone who parts from me is thrown away like a useless branch and withers. Such branches are gathered into a pile to be burned. But if you stay joined to me and my*

*words remain in you, you may ask any request you like, and
it will be granted! My true disciples produce much fruit. This
brings great glory to my Father.* (John 15:1, 4–8)

Each brushstroke expresses how Jesus—the true Vine—is the Source of everything we need in life. As the branches, we find our very life in Him. And it is only in vital connection with Him that we grow, find nourishment and fulfillment, and live productive lives.

> We become malnourished and stunted when we connect to a different branch and try to get from it what the true Vine alone can provide.

We become malnourished and stunted when we connect to a different branch and try to get from it what the true Vine alone can provide. Separation from God results in huge disappointments and an utter lack of soul satisfaction. Even the most noble, well-intentioned parents, spouses, and friends can't love us the way we were created to be loved—perfectly, by a perfect Lover.

It was in my isolation that I learned this truth. Prayer became a new priority for me. I carved out time every day to journal my thoughts, to talk to God, and to listen for what He might have to say in response. I did my journaling every morning while my baby napped, but the conversation with God often continued throughout the day.

Isolation Opens Our Eyes to Recognize God's Presence

Kendall, who was four at the time, had been plagued by a stubborn plantar wart. We had experienced several traumatic encounters with the doctor in an attempt to rid her of it, but the thing just wouldn't die. One Tuesday morning, Kendall complained again about the discomfort the wart was causing her, so I picked up the phone and called the doctor to schedule another appointment. Kendall was less than thrilled. Having the wart burned off was very painful. The doctor probably wasn't thrilled, either. Kendall's screams during previous treatments had probably sent some of his waiting patients in search of a new family doctor.

I made the appointment anyway. As I hung up the phone, God spoke to me. I sensed His message more than heard it. But it was as clear as any communication I have ever received, and I knew it was His voice.

He said, "Why don't you ask Me to heal the wart?" And then again, "Why don't you and Kendall pray and ask Me to heal the wart?"

Being the great woman of faith that I was, I said, "But, God, what if we pray and You don't heal her? Won't that damage her faith?"

You know, I could almost hear Him chuckling. He said, "Don't worry about Me. I can handle My own reputation."

I thought He had a good point, so we prayed. Each night, when I tucked Kendall into bed, we simply asked God to heal her wart. And then, with my daughter safely asleep, I would go down to my little office, where I did most of my praying, and almost blow the roof off. "Oh, God, You've got to come through this time, not so much for her foot but for her faith."

On Tuesday and Wednesday we prayed. On Thursday afternoon, Kendall came running into my room and said, "Look, Mommy, look!" And there on her foot where the wart had been was this little crater. The wart had simply fallen off. I was so moved that God cared enough about a little girl named Kendall and a mommy named Donna that He would speak to me. He wanted my friendship that much.

But I was still struggling emotionally. One day I wrote the following words in my journal: "God, I am really hurting...and I need a touch from You today." And then I sat in the stillness, waiting to hear what God might say.

The doorbell's ring punctured the silence. Again, being the great woman of faith that I was, I found myself annoyed by the interruption. I went to open the door. Standing there, to my surprise, was Marilyn, a casual friend from church. She stayed only a moment, after delivering a bouquet of flowers and a hug. I was warmed by her kind gesture. I put the flowers in a vase filled with water and then settled in again with my journal to resume waiting on God. Glancing down at my journal, I read the words I'd written not ten minutes before: "God, I am really hurting...and I need a touch from You today." I realized then that God, who lives in my friend Marilyn, had just shown up at my front door with a bouquet of flowers and a hug.

Nothing compares to friendship with God. Was I still lonely? Yes. But I had found something more precious than any human relationship. I had learned about God, prayed to Him, and worshipped Him my whole life, but it wasn't until I had no one else that I came to know Him as a Friend.

Meeting daily with God became a nonnegotiable practice in my life, like taking a shower or nursing the baby. Whatever else I needed to have happen on any given day needed to happen around my time alone with God. Before my season of isolation, it had been the other way around.

Once I started giving my friendship with God the priority it was due, and once our relationship was firmly established, He gave me Patty, and what a blessing she has been! But I never want to go back to the way it was when I allowed other relationships to take precedence over my best Friend—the only one I know will never let me down.

Invest in an ever-deepening friendship with God by spending time with Him daily. Ask Him to show you how to build health and intimacy into your primary relationships. Then, look for a friend with whom you can share the adventure.

WHEN YOU CAN'T FIND A FRIEND

Questions for Reflection and Discussion

1. Reflecting on the relationships you have had throughout life, can you identify any tendencies in yourself that have been detrimental to establishing and/or maintaining friendships?

2. Do you ever struggle with self-worth? Why? What qualities do you possess that could enrich another person in a relationship? Be generous with yourself and name them.

3. Brainstorm some ways in which you might find a new friend and also how you could invite her into a friendship once you have found her.

4. We discussed a passage from John 15 in which Jesus compared His relationship with us to that of a vine and its branches. Which other branch(es) have you tried attaching yourself to instead of the true Vine? What have been the consequences of that attachment?

5. Think back to a period of loneliness or friendlessness in your life. Might God have had a lesson for you to learn through that time? If so, what was it?

6. Do you consider God to be a friend? If not, what would it take for you to invite Him into your life?

10

THE PERFECT FRIEND

Anyone who hangs around the evangelical church community long enough will hear talk about "inviting Jesus into our lives." This is a good thing. But infinitely more wonderful is the truth that God is inviting *us* into *His* life. The whole Bible is the story of God's radical plan to restore His lost relationship with His rebellious people—you and me. And if we can somehow see the story unfold with fresh eyes, we will be amazed at the lengths to which He was willing to go and the price that He was willing to pay for the joy of our presence at His table for all eternity.

It's Amazing What Some Will Do for Love

I married my high-school sweetheart. We became friends in the church youth group because we shared common interests, like tormenting our youth leaders and Sunday school teachers with playful pranks. Neither of us intended for our friendship to become a romance—Randy because he had just been emancipated from a relationship that he had found quite stifling, and I because I was corresponding with an "older man" who was away at college.

At some point, probably in the getaway car during one of our capers, we began to notice the sparks between us. I loved his wacky sense of humor and respected his passion for God. With all the wisdom of a fifteen-year-old, I could definitely see the potential of a future with this young man.

One day, I found out that our youth group was planning a skiing trip to nearby Banff. I couldn't ski because of my "trick knees," but I hated the thought of missing out on the adventure.

"Wouldn't it be fun to drive up to Banff in the afternoon, swim in the Sulphur Mountain hot springs, and meet the rest of the group for supper?" I asked Randy. He thought it was a great idea. Unfortunately, though, he was scheduled to work. He said that he'd try to trade shifts. In the meantime, I recruited a carful of other kids to come along.

Randy asked everyone he could think of at work to trade shifts with him. No one agreed to. Finally, in desperation, he got down on one knee before a guy who had already declined and said, "Please, man? This is for love!"

The guy paused, then said, "Okay, but here's how it's going to work. You'll work my shift for me and give me the money."

"Yeah, okay," Randy said.

"Then," the other guy continued, "I'll work your shift and keep the money."

"Hold it, hold it, hold it," Randy said, waving a hand in the guy's face. "Let me get this straight. You work my shift, and you get the money. Then, I work your shift, and you get the money."

"Right," the guy confirmed.

"It's a deal!" Randy said.

Isn't it amazing what some people will do for love?

Of course, I didn't know any of this until Randy shared it with me years later. I do know, however, that we had a wonderful, romantic day together in Banff (with four of our closest friends), and I do remember that it was during the drive home that Randy held my hand for the first time. It was the first bud of a romance that has blossomed continually for more than thirty years. Randy remembers the exact spot on the Trans-Canada Highway where he finally worked up the nerve to take my hand in his. And to this day, every time we travel that section of road, he takes it again.

As much as I appreciate the sacrifice that Randy made to be with me that day, there are, of course, people who give up much more for the sake of the ones they love.

The Staggering Cost of Love

Most mothers remember the mild (or major) sense of panic they felt the first time they sent their little ones off to school. So much is at risk. The school bus could crash. The teacher might be mean. There could be bullies or drug pushers on the playground. Anything could happen.

How must the Father have felt as He stood on heaven's threshold and said farewell to His Son just before He stepped across the galaxies to this troubled planet? The omnipotent Creator, reduced to a human fetus. God with skin on. The One whose mere words were the catalyst for the formation of the stars and planets becomes one who cannot articulate a single word. The One whose breath could level forests becomes one whose cry is barely audible above the lowing of cattle and the bleating of sheep. The One who provided sources of food for the earth's inhabitants becomes one who cannot even feed Himself. The One accustomed to the worship of angels slips into time and turmoil unnoticed.

Almost. Heaven's adversary is paying attention. Immediately, the serpent rears his head and danger hovers nearby. Beginning at the manger and ending at the cross, evil pursues Him. Anything could happen.

It's amazing what some will do for love.

What a bold risk. What incredible carelessness. Whoever heard of a God who loves so passionately, so recklessly? A god who creates or destroys, yes. A god who demands and rages, certainly. A god like Shiva, the Hindu god, who is allegedly pleased by the practice of widow burning, or the ancient god Molech, who demanded the sacrifice of living children by fire. But a God who loves enough to lower Himself to be one of us? To embrace poverty and helplessness? To play by His own rules to the point of dying, because He would rather die than live without us? Who ever heard of such love? Until Jesus, no one!

Why would God take such a risk and so recklessly endanger His one and only Son? It was for love. It was because God's great heart yearns for your friendship and mine, like an abandoned lover, a heartbroken father, a grief-stricken friend. And as long as there is any hope of restoration, He cannot rest.

> Why would God take such a risk and so recklessly endanger His one and only Son? It was for love.

This is why He launched the most extreme rescue mission ever attempted, with no guarantee of a positive outcome. Having risked so much, still He allows us the dignity of choice. We can choose to accept His offer of friendship or not. God places His great heart in our corrupt and careless hands. We have the power to grievously wound the heart of almighty God. We can reject Him. The choice is ours. Yet His desperation to restore His relationship with humanity drove Him to hazard the risk. Jesus temporarily resigned His rightful position as God of the universe and walked away from wealth and worship to participate fully in our experience by becoming one of us. He entered a world of pain and poverty, of death and despair, of hunger and hopelessness.

> *Though he was God, he did not demand and cling to his rights as God. He made himself nothing; he took the humble position of a slave and appeared in human form. And in human form he obediently humbled himself even further by dying a criminal's death on a cross.*   (Philippians 2:6–8)

The baby Jesus grew up into the God-man who laughed and loved and cried but never sinned; the Galilean carpenter who swung a hammer, healed the sick, and washed feet. The splendor and safety of heaven were left behind—God wagered it all in the wild hope that His love will be returned, not rejected. But in God's sovereignty and wisdom, the danger, the dark side of Christmas, becomes Good Friday.

And the great God of heaven stretches out His arms against a rough, wooden beam to be tortured to death by those for whom His heart aches with love. With each stab of the thorns into His scalp, each blow grinding metal stakes through bone and flesh, Jesus writhes in agony and remembers that, in some distant place, He and the Father designed the human body: these very muscles, nerves, and membranes that now cry out in excruciating pain.

As He hangs there, struggling for every agonizing breath, He chooses *this*. He isn't powerless. He has chosen to lay aside His power for love. Angels hover nearby, waiting for the command that they believe surely must come—the command to rescue the Son of God and destroy the world. "How dare they?" the angels ask, indignant. "How dare these created ones treat their Messiah like this?" But the command never comes. Jesus chooses this horrible death out of love.

But the physical suffering and the humiliation are only the beginning. Jesus begins to feel dirty. The sin and evil of every generation of humankind begin to wash over the uncorrupted Son of God, and He must face His Father...like this. Somehow Jesus, the only sinless Man, hangs condemned of every rape, child molestation, murder, theft, and lie. The Father's pent-up wrath surges out with the force of a tidal wave. Jesus endures the punishment for all.

> It is because Jesus knew separation from the Father that I never have to. It is because Jesus was forsaken that I never will be. And you need not be, either.

The Father's stored rage spent, He turns His back on His only Son, who hangs drowning in a cesspool of sin. Jesus cries, "Father, why have You forsaken me?" And the perfect, eternal friendship between the Father and the Son is rent in two. It is because Jesus knew separation from the Father that I never have to. It is because Jesus was forsaken that I never will be. And you need not be, either.

"Greater love has no one than this, that he lay down his life for his friends" (John 15:13 NIV). *"This is how we know what love is: Jesus Christ laid down his life for us"* (1 John 3:16 NIV). It's amazing what some people will do for love.

How Should We Respond?

If that kind of love doesn't rock your world, you must be unconscious. No one else can love you like that. No one but Jesus can offer you that kind of friendship. Taking hold of His outstretched, nail-scarred hand as you walk through life changes everything. It won't guarantee an easy life. But Jesus does promise us a fulfilling life. He said, *"My purpose is to give life in all its fullness"* (John 10:10).

I saw this fullness demonstrated amazingly in the life of Brian, Sonja's widower, in the months before and after he lost his wife.

Seize the "Fullness of Life" Jesus Offers

I have always regretted that I never had a chance to express to Sonja my heart's promise—that I would do my best to take care of her family after she was gone. I have, however, done my best to keep that promise. Brian and the boys were at our home often, especially during the first year following her death, and it was so gratifying to watch my daughter Kendall become close friends with my best friend's twin sons.

Brian felt free to call and ask to come over for what he called "hot tub therapy." Brian, Randy, and I would sit in our hot tub, processing our grief together, till we were positively pruny. We mostly listened to Brian talk about everything he was dealing with as a single dad.

But here's the amazing part. In the days just before Sonja's death and in the weeks that followed, Brian marveled at one thing: how he had spent the years following Sonja's diagnosis of cancer living in fear of losing her. Anytime she was sick with the flu, he would wonder, *Is this the end?* He would cling to her, weeping, and say, "Please don't leave me. I can't do this without you." Yet, when she lay dying, he felt no such sense of helpless desperation. In its place was the peace of God.

Brian didn't have the grace to walk through the valley of the shadow of death until he actually got there. When it was finally time to walk through that valley, he had no fear, only the calm assurance of the presence of God and the deep heart knowledge that He never takes us beyond the place where His grace can sustain us.

Brian's situation was pretty extreme. Maybe you're not in that place. Your life is pretty good. You've never really worried about what you would cling to if your world fell apart, and you don't intend to think about it now.

Nicky Gumbel, who developed the Alpha course to convey the basics of the Christian faith, tells the story of the day, decades ago, when his family purchased their first TV set. The picture wasn't very clear. In fact, it was sort of like looking through a window at a blizzard outside. The vertical hold was a bit off, too, but they were delighted with their new acquisition. It wasn't until a friend came to visit that they learned there was something wrong. "You need an antenna on that thing, and then you'll get clearer reception," they were told. So, they went out and got an antenna and were amazed at the difference it made in the picture. They were also amazed that they had been satisfied to settle for the poor quality they'd had previously.

> I wouldn't trade my friendship with Jesus for anything, because what I have with Him is priceless.

My friend Patty looks back on her life before she accepted Jesus' invitation of friendship in much the same way. She says it was like walking around asleep. She didn't know what she was missing because she had no basis of comparison. But ever since accepting Jesus, she has often said, "I wouldn't want to live one second of my life without Him. Not one second."

And neither would I. I wouldn't trade my friendship with Jesus for anything, because what I have with Him is priceless—the knowledge that no matter what happens to me, now or in the future, I am not, nor will I ever be, without hope. God is with me, and He will never fail me. Life's hurts, struggles, and pressures cannot crush me.

Accept His Invitation of Friendship

If you know Jesus personally, you are never without hope. Do you live in the fullness of that promise?

If you've never entered into friendship with Him, why haven't you? What would prevent you from doing so today? It simply requires a sincere heart and a simple expression of a few words that are necessary in every friendship: *sorry, thank you,* and *please.*

To enter into a relationship with God, we must express to Him our awareness that we have wronged Him by living independently of Him and making selfish choices, and that we are sorry for having done so. We also need to acknowledge His incredible sacrifice in sending His Son to die a horrible death on a Roman cross to satisfy the demands of justice for our wrongs. Out of a heart of gratitude, we say, "Thank You, Jesus."

Then we surrender control to Him. Knowing that His way is always best, we say, "Please take over the leadership of my life."

And then, we grow in intimacy with Him, the way we would in relationship with any friend. Spending time together, talking and listening, laughing, loving, crying, and simply "doing life" together is what it's all about. If you've never taken the step of inviting Jesus into your life, please don't put this book down until you have. I promise that you will never, ever regret it.

Maybe you began a relationship with Jesus at some point but never made it beyond the excitement of spring and summer. Maybe you're facing an autumn of disappointment with God over some loss in your life. If this is the case, let me encourage you to go back to Him. Allow Him to walk with you through the pain to a place where you can enjoy the comfort and intimacy of a mature faith.

That is what Simon Peter did. He was Jesus' friend, but Jesus was doing and saying some pretty strange things—things that Peter and the others didn't understand. They were disappointed, and many of them walked away. Jesus must have felt wounded. He knew His friends were abandoning Him. He looked over His shoulder, and Peter was still there. Jesus asked, "Are you going to leave Me, too?"

I love Peter's response. He said, "Where would we go? You alone have the words that give eternal life. We believe them, and we know You are the Holy One of God." (See John 6:66–69.) I think the cry of Peter's heart was this: "Lord, I don't understand You, and some of the calls You make seem like nonsense to me. But I know You are who You say You are, and that's enough for me. You are God, and You are my Friend!"

In the midst of your pain and disappointment, let this be the cry of your heart and, in time, Jesus will fill all the crevices in your faith with Himself.

If your faith is vibrant and growing, take a minute to let the familiar story of God's extreme love fill you with wonder once again. It is so easy to take for granted this amazing reality—that we can share a friendship with the great God of heaven. As in any friendship, we can go deeper only by spending time together. What an amazing privilege it is to be able to meet with God, anytime, anywhere! He is always ready and willing to commune with us. Talk to Him. Listen to Him. Worship Him. Then, pray with me:

> Praise to You, dear Jesus, King of Kings and Lord of Lords! You are above all, sovereign and omnipotent. Thank You for choosing to use Your power to become powerless. Thank You for the wisdom and love that drove You to become a sovereign victim, so that I could become Your friend.

THE PERFECT FRIEND

Questions for Reflection and Discussion

1. Did anything about Donna's description of God's radical rescue mission make you think differently about Jesus' love for you? Explore those thoughts.

2. How does walking through life in relationship with God change the quality of a person's life? (See John 10:10.) If you have invited Jesus into your life, how has His friendship changed things for you?

3. Most believers feel disappointed with God at some point in their lives. This sense of disillusionment is not caused by God's failure but by our faulty perspective. How might these periods of disappointment be different if we were to take the approach of the apostle Peter in John 6:66–69?

4. We discussed the importance of saying "Sorry," "Thank You," and "Please" to God. If you have never invited Jesus to be your

friend, why not make today the day you express to Him those words that are necessary in all friendships?

5. How can you begin growing in intimacy with God?

CONCLUSION

Sonja wrote this poem for me when we were in junior high. To read it, you almost believe that she knew her time on this earth would be brief.

A ray of sunshine on a cloudy day.
You give me joy.
I tell you all my sorrows,
my secrets,
my dreams.

You understand.
You laugh with me,
cry with me
and
pray with me.

And you never tire.
>You never say no when I want to talk.
I often yell and seem impatient…but please
>don't think it's because I don't care.
The love I have for you is as deep as
>anything between two friends can be.

People say someday we'll
drift
  apart.

Maybe that's true.
>But in our hearts, we'll always
>>be close together.

Our paths may separate,
>we'll go our different ways, but
>>one day we'll meet again in a
place far from here
a place made especially for friends
>with dreams and
for other people who love each other as
>much as
>>I love you.

—Sonja

The last time I spoke to Sonja was the day she learned she was dying. In spite of the valiant efforts of a fine team of doctors, there was nothing left to be done. Many of her vital organs were shutting down, including her kidneys.

As a result, she could drink very little, and she was always thirsty. The day she said good-bye to her three sons, Caleb,

Daniel, and Michael, she told them she was going to heaven to have a "Big Gulp" with Jesus. As I drove the boys home from the hospital the day she passed away, we remembered what she had said and imagined her doing just that.

I hadn't been planning to go to the hospital that day. No one had expected the end to come so quickly. But God knew that I needed to be there—to say good-bye, embrace her lifeless form, and weep with Brian and the boys.

In the moments when Brian and I were the only ones left in Sonja's room, Brian hugged me and said, "Thank you for leading that twelve-year-old girl to Jesus. She's in heaven now because of your friendship." Through my tears, I said, "Thank you for being such a good husband to my friend."

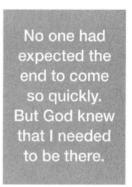

No one had expected the end to come so quickly. But God knew that I needed to be there.

Joining us in the room shortly after this was one of our pastors, along with the boys; Sonja's mom, Bonnie; and her sister, Paula. We stood around the bed, held hands, and thanked God for Sonja's life—a life lived with courage and compassion; a life well-lived. We committed her to God's keeping and pleaded for comfort and strength for those she had left behind.

Some days, it was hard to decide which was more difficult: dealing with my own grief or watching Brian and the boys deal with theirs. Brian had such a hard time imagining what the future held for him. He could envision his sons graduating, going on to college, marrying, and raising families, but his own future was just a big blank page. He couldn't picture himself alone, but he couldn't picture himself with anyone else, either.

The first conversation Randy and I had with Brian about the possibility of his marrying again occurred during a session of "hot tub therapy" and ended with Brian's emphatic pronouncement: "The first time someone tries to fix me up with another woman, there's going to be blood on the wall." Yet, over the months following Sonja's death, we watched him pass the point of "I'm so lonely!" and progress to "I have all this love to give…I need somebody to love."

Not long after Brian reached this stage, he began to notice a name that recurred in his conversations. It came up both at work and when he was among friends, and he was having more and more trouble getting it out of his mind. It was the name of a woman he and Sonja had known casually for many years—someone they had appreciated and respected. Brian later learned that many people had been privately thinking about him in relation to this woman, but what Brian alone knew was that, before she died, Sonja had expressed much the same thought. In fact, she'd even told him, "When I'm gone, you should marry someone like Darlene."

Darlene had grown up in a loving family environment. All her life, she'd wanted nothing more than to marry, have a bunch of kids, and nurture them in the same way that she had been nurtured as a child. In high school, when her classmates were trying to figure out what was next, Darlene really didn't have big career aspirations. She just wanted a family. It never occurred to her that the desires of her romantic young heart would not be fulfilled.

With no prospective husbands on the immediate horizon, she worked for a year and then went off to Bible college, where the idea of a career in the church began to appeal to her. As she became more and more passionate about church ministry, an ideal vision of her future began to come into focus. She wanted to marry a man who would share her passion for ministry. Together they would pour their lives into their family and their church.

As graduation approached, however, there was still no suitable man in the picture, and Darlene wrestled again with the question, "Now what?" All she knew for sure was that her deepest desires were for a husband and, eventually, children.

Over the next several years, Darlene worked in church-related jobs as an administrative assistant, always feeling that her life was not quite complete. Finally, a new job in Toronto put her in the right place at the right time to begin a dating relationship that she hoped would lead to marriage. Life was good. For the first time in years, her dreams of having a family of her own were within reach.

One New Year's Eve, as Darlene sat in church and listened to the sermon, her pastor made the following statement: "God often breaks into our lives when we least expect it and sets us on a new course." She sensed that God was about to do this for her. Right then and there, she promised that if He did, she would follow His leading.

What she didn't know was that following God's leading would mean ending the relationship she'd believed was the answer to a lifetime of longing; that it would mean the death of the dream of getting married and having children. Nearly thirty years old, Darlene felt that this might have been her last chance. Yet, as painful as it was, she knew deep down that this relationship was not one God intended to be "till death do us part."

Determined to obey God's direction for her life, Darlene responded to His prompting to move back to Calgary, where she joined the staff of a large church as the children's pastor. Darlene loved working with children, but doing so only increased her long-ing to have kids of her own, even as time marched relentlessly toward the end of her child-bearing years. There were times when she struggled with God, saying, "You created me for this, and You gave me these desires. Why aren't You fulfilling them?" It was a very lonely and painful journey.

> Darlene decided to open herself up to the creative ways in which she thought God might fulfill her desires.

But Darlene decided to open herself up to the creative ways in which she thought God might fulfill those desires. This quest led her to Germany, where she became a dorm mother for children whose parents were serving as missionaries in Eastern Europe, Russia, and the Middle East. There, she had the privilege of living with, loving, and helping raise eighteen children for three years. God used this experience to give Darlene an outlet for her mothering instincts, and through it, she came to realize that she could deeply love children who were not her own and, in so doing, find contentment.

Three years later, Darlene found herself back in Toronto, working as an administrative assistant once again.

Coincidentally, as some might say, I was attending the church in Calgary where she had formerly served as children's pastor. Brian was on staff at the church, working with my brother-in-law, Jason, in the area of music and worship arts. One day, Darlene called all the way from Toronto to ask Jason, whom she knew from working at the church, a question relating to a project she was involved in. Jason, knowing that Brian had greater expertise in her area of interest, made it a conference call, and boy met girl.

Actually, Brian and Darlene were already acquaintances at the time and had many friends in common. But, in the wake of this phone call, Brian couldn't get Darlene out of his head. Hundreds of miles away, Darlene was having trouble getting him out of hers. She knew about his loss, though, and whenever he came to mind, she tried turning her thoughts into prayers for him and his three teenage sons.

Meanwhile, during another session of "hot tub therapy," Brian expounded on all the reasons why no one would ever be romantically interested in him again. "Who would ever be attracted to a graying, forty-year-old man with three teenage sons?" he mused aloud. "It would be like asking a woman to move into the boys' dorm. Beyond that, who would want to marry a pastor and live under the microscope of ministry?"

I'll let Brian tell you the next part of the story himself.

During this same period of time, the boys and I take a few days to go skiing and to look ahead at 2002. In the words of one of the guys, "It can't be worse than last year." Over dinner one night, we begin to talk about how they might feel if I were to end up in another relationship. In the course of this, we say, "Let's make a list of attributes. We can dream and be really demanding at this point because there's no one in sight." Ideas come on the table, such as: she must love God; she must be a better cook than Dad (!); she should understand something about Germany, because that's been such a big part of our lives; she shouldn't want to replace Mom; etc. Then we laugh and say, "Well, let's see what God does with that list!"

Close to the end of January, I still can't get Darlene out of my head, and so now I've got to figure out what to do with that. In my mind, the person I've been think-ing about is the most eligible woman in the whole denomination, so I'm sure she's involved in a relationship with someone else. If that's the case, then all of this wondering is a waste of time. Somehow I've got to find out if she's "available." Once again, after some further hot tub sessions with Donna and Randy Carter and Jason and his wife, Jocelyn, I decide to authorize some "research."

It so happens that Darlene's best friend, Colleen, is in Calgary and goes to First Alliance Church and sings in one of our worship teams with her husband, Randy. So, a phone call is made between Jocelyn and Colleen. This has now deteriorated to the level of a bad junior-high romance with friends calling friends to see if somebody likes somebody else. Unbelievable! At first, Colleen is very guarded. Her friend has been the subject of too many matchmaking attempts, and she wants to protect her. Then she asks, "Who wants to know?" and my name is mentioned.

A week goes by, and I see Colleen at church. I feel that I need to tell her that I at least know she's had an interesting phone call. That's when Colleen lets me know that she's already let "someone" know that I was asking about her, albeit indirectly. At this point, I feel concerned, because "someone" has already been waiting for a week, and I haven't done anything! So now it's serious. I need to hear from God about what to do. I take the next two days, Sunday and Monday, to pray and fast. On Monday at lunch, I'm in the prayer chapel at church and clearly sense God telling me, "You haven't begun to imagine how good life can be yet. Trust Me."

And so the next day, I find myself before the biggest blank computer screen I have ever seen. How can I begin to communicate with her? What will she think? With a lump in my throat and my heart pounding all the way up to my head, I hit "send" and off it goes.

What I learned later is that Darlene had also set aside the same time to fast and pray, and that, once she received my message, God clearly said to her, "My child, this is who you have been waiting for. Let Brian be an expression of My love for you. Trust Me."

That's when the romance began in earnest. Hot tub therapy was cut short because Brian always seemed to have a phone call to make. Within a few weeks, Brian decided to fly out to Toronto because, in his words, "I have to look into that girl's eyes." Darlene picked him up at the airport and took him to a coffee shop, where they shared their first kiss. Afterward, they walked out of the coffee shop and right into a jewelry store.

God clearly said to her, "My child, this is who you have been waiting for. Let Brian be an expression of My love for you."

When Brian came home from Toronto, he introduced Darlene to his sons with a photo that had been taken of her while she was a dorm mother in Germany—at the same school the boys had attended. In the picture, she was hugging two of their best friends. I don't think she could have found better references.

A few weeks later, Darlene flew out to Calgary to meet the boys, and the next day she was engaged. She and Brian were married three months later. Before she made her wedding vows to Brian, Darlene made vows to the boys, among them this promise: "I will always honor your mother's memory and I will never try to replace her." There wasn't a dry eye in the place.

Who but God could have placed Darlene in all the same settings as Brian and his boys so that they would know all the same people and have so many common friends? What are the chances that they would both work, at different times, in Toronto, at First Alliance Church in Calgary, and for the same ministry in Liel, Germany? Who but God could have prepared Darlene to nurture Sonja's children so beautifully?

It's as if Brian and Darlene had been on two separate but destined-to-converge paths for forty years. As Brian put it, "I continue to marvel at the wonderful gift God has been preparing for me literally for years."

I know Darlene feels the same. These are her words:

I believe strongly and with more conviction than at any other point in my life that the God I love, the God that loves me, is a sovereign God, He is a good God, and His love and grace are available to us in the good times and in the hard times. Would I have chosen for the man I love, his wife, Sonja, and their children to walk through a twelve-year journey of suffering? No. Would I have chosen to be alone for twenty-plus years? No. Do I now understand some of the whys I asked over the years? Yes. I believe that when God fashioned me in my mother's womb, He created me for Brian and the boys, for this period in their lives.

When Darlene went to buy a bridal gown, the saleswoman gasped in horror and exclaimed, "You want it for *this* August?" She was appalled that Darlene was planning a wedding with only a few months' notice. But how could that woman have known that God had been preparing this bride her whole life?

I have had a front-row seat watching this new family come together, and God's hand in the process has been unmistakable.

But I often wonder how best to fulfill my promise to Sonja during this stage of their journey. I have asked myself, *What would I want from my best friend after I was gone?* I think I would want two things: for her to do everything she could to help my family take the steps through the inevitable changes connected with moving on, and to keep my memory alive for my children.

There are times when these two goals seem to be contradictory. In fact, there are many strange paradoxes related to the process of remembering the past and moving on toward the future. Darlene constantly struggles to reconcile the paradoxical reality that her greatest happiness has come out of her family's greatest sorrow.

One evening, while my husband, who was to be Brian's best man, and I visited over coffee with the couple and listened to them talk about their wedding plans, I teared up unexpectedly. I was overwhelmed with opposing emotions—so happy for Brian to be entering a joyful new chapter of life; so pleased that the boys had received Darlene with open arms, even as their hearts continued to heal from the pain of losing their mother; so glad that Darlene would know what it is to be loved wholeheartedly by a good man; and yet so terribly sad that Sonja no longer played an active role in the unfolding story of this family.

Later that night, I said to Darlene, "I'm so sad that Sonja is gone, but I'm so glad that you are here."

It sounded strange, even to me, but that's what was on my heart.

Fulfilling my promise to Sonja has meant learning the balance of embracing the future and honoring the past. I don't get it right all the time, but Darlene has been very gracious, even though it must be awkward at times for her to hear all the "Sonja stories."

She understands the importance of keeping Sonja's memory alive for the boys.

Many sad days have followed Sonja's death. There are sad moments still. And there are moments that are bittersweet, such as watching Sonja's son Michael and my daughter Kendall—best friends since childhood—fall in love. And then, when they got engaged, seeing Kendall wear Sonja's engagement diamond set in a new ring. There was the moment Brian clutched Darlene's hand as Randy walked Kendall down the aisle, and the moments when we all paid tribute to Sonja during the reception that followed. There is the joy of knowing that Mike and Kendall are taking our story of friendship into the future. But, more than that, there is the solace of knowing that Sonja is with her best Friend, Jesus, and that she is more whole, alive, and content than she ever was on earth. There is the joyful assurance that we will see her again, in Sonja's words, "in a place made especially for friends."

If your life ended suddenly, who would keep your memory alive?

As we conclude our discussion of friendship, let me ask you a question. If your life ended suddenly, who would keep your memory alive? Is there anyone who knows you well enough, loves you deeply enough, and is committed enough? If you had to choose a group of pallbearers today, who would they be? Is there a circle of friends whom you can count on to stand by you in life and to carry you in death?

And do you share a friendship with the One who longs to be everyone's best Friend? I hope so. If not, I hope you will invite Him into your life and invest your time and energy in becoming His friend. Devote yourself to growing a mature relationship of love, trust, and accountability with the best Friend who ever lived. I believe that, in time, He will also give you a human friend with whom you share affinity and who is available and authentic. A friend with whom you can be at ease; a friend who extends affirmation, acceptance, accountability, and assistance. The kind of friend who will come into your life, stay awhile, and leave footprints on your heart.

CONCLUSION

Questions for Reflection and Discussion

1. Darlene struggled with God over the "whys" of life as they related to her desire to have a family of her own. She asked God, "You created me for this, and You gave me these desires. Why aren't You fulfilling them?" Can you relate to that kind of struggle? What are some of the "whys" of your life?

2. How do Darlene's words on page 194 (reprinted below) speak into your struggles?

   I believe strongly and with more conviction than any other point in my life that the God I love, the God that loves me, is a sovereign God, He is a good God, and His love and grace are available to us in the good times and in the hard times. Would I have chosen for the man I love, his wife, Sonja, and their children to walk through a twelve-year journey of suffering? No. Would I have chosen to be alone for twenty-plus years? No. Do I now understand some of the whys I asked over the years? Yes. I believe that when God fashioned me in my mother's womb, He created me for Brian and the boys, for this period in their lives.

3. Donna wrote, "I have had a front-row seat watching this new family come together, and God's hand in it has been unmistakable." In what ways has God's hand been present in weaving together the circumstances in your life? Is it possible you have attributed to luck or coincidence what was, in reality, God's active participation in your life?

4. If your life was suddenly taken from you, who loves you deeply enough to keep your memory alive?

5. Do you share a deepening friendship with God?

CHERISHED PHOTOS
FROM THE AUTHOR'S ALBUMS

Donna (left) and Sonja in their early teens, posing with a couple of Mounties.

Donna's sister Debbie, Donna, friend Carol, sister Jocelyn, and Sonja on Donna and Randy's wedding day, June 19, 1981.

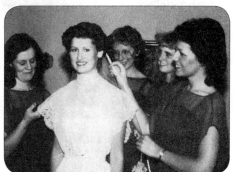

Donna with Sonja (left) the day she married Brian, one month after Donna had married Randy.

Brian, Caleb, Sonja, and the miracle babies, Michael and Daniel.

Darlene's first Carter/Delamont camping trip. She is a brave woman!

Kendall and the twins,
together as always.

Mike and Kendall—a prophetic picture, perhaps?

Darlene and Brian on their wedding day.

Mike, Kendall, cousin Jon Delamont, and Daniel at Brian and Darlene's wedding reception.

The family adventures continue.

Brian, Darlene, Donna, and Randy at the wedding of their children Michael and Kendall.

Mike and Kendall, wearing Sonja's diamond, on their wedding day.

ABOUT THE AUTHOR

Donna Carter has a unique ability to synthesize life experience into digestible life lessons. She is sought as a speaker across the globe because of her clarity and humor, as well as the lightbulb moments she triggers for people seeking help on their spiritual journeys.

Her first book, *10 Smart Things Women Can Do to Build a Better Life*, was released in the fall of 2007 and is now being distributed in five countries. The DVD life management course by the same name is an outreach tool that is working its way around the world, making appearances in Islamic countries, developing nations, and communist countries, as well as U.S. military bases.

Donna has traveled widely and is passionate about social justice, especially helping women and children achieve their full potential. Her recent adventures include connecting with the underground church in China, experiencing the catastrophic earthquake in Haiti, and linking Canadian women with young mothers living in abject poverty in El Salvador through Compassion International.

Donna and her husband, Randy, are the cofounders of Straight Talk Ministries, a nonprofit organization committed to helping people find faith and apply it to everyday life. They live in Calgary, a thriving city in the shadow of the Canadian Rockies. Donna and Randy have two young adult daughters and a newly acquired son-in-law.

Formerly an interior designer by profession, Donna has decided to devote the rest of her career life to helping people live purposefully through her speaking and writing.

Donna may be contacted for speaking engagements at www.donnacarter.org.

⌣

A portion of the proceeds of this book have been designated to Compassion's Child Survival Program–ES 21 in El Salvador.

To join Donna in reaching out to children in the developing world through Compassion International, visit www.compassion.com (for residents of the United States) or compassion.ca (for residents of Canada).